LITERATURE AND FILM

LITERATURE

AND FILM

ROBERT RICHARDSON

Indiana University Press

BLOOMINGTON / LONDON

Published in Canada by Fitzhenry & Whiteside Limited, Don Mills, Ontario

Library of Congress catalog card number: 72–85098
Standard Book Number: 253–14845–6
Manufactured in the United States of America

To my father

Contents

Acknowledgments

I HAVE DEALT VERY LITTLE WITH DRAMA AND THE film, largely because Allardyce Nicoll did the job so well in his *Film and Theatre* in 1936. My debts are heavy, indeed they are pervasive and past listing. The notes at the end of the volume document only a part of what I owe to others. I lay claim to little originality beyond that of emphasis and I trust that my particularly extensive obligations to Balázs, to Eisenstein, to Agee, and especially to Vachel Lindsay are perfectly clear. I must also thank John Williams for his initial support in this undertaking, and for permission to use material that originally appeared in *The Denver Quarterly*. And to my other colleagues, Gerald Chapman, Burton Feldman, and Edward Twining, I owe a great debt for sane and perceptive criticism though it would be unfair to hold them to account for my lapses. I should also like to thank Mrs. Sheila Steinberg for her patient and alert editing of the manuscript. Finally, I do not know how to thank my wife, Elizabeth, whose gentle arts of creative forbearance make everything possible.

LITERATURE AND FILM

Prologue

IT IS BECOMING INCREASINGLY CLEAR THAT ANY attempt to assess the important arts of our time will have to consider both modern literature and the film. This volume contends, further, that the connections that exist between literature and film are worth concentrating upon first and most simply because literature and film are near neighbors in many respects and secondly because these two forms of artistic expression appear to be increasingly dominant in the formation of modern aesthetic responses.

It has been obvious since at least the time of D. W. Griffith that literature has had a considerable influence on the film, and at the same time it is equally clear, though much less a matter for discussion, that the film has had important repercussions in literature and has even been in some ways, a major influence on modern writing. Beyond this, it can be argued that film form and literary form have certain strong similarities and that film technique and literary technique are often parallel. I would also argue that literary criticism and film criticism can each benefit from the other. Film consciousness gently urges the reader of literature to fresh alertness to the visual and aural qualities that mark much great writing, and literary training gives depth and perspective to one's appreciation of film.

The overarching likeness that makes it possible to consider most films and much of literature together is the very simple but possibly crucial observation that, in general, literature and film are storytelling arts. From this the technician argues that they have narrative in common, and the humanist notes that they are by that token committed to making themselves intelligible. The plan of this book is accordingly as simple as its double subject and double interest will permit. After a sketch of the subject, there are two chapters which look for literary backgrounds and influences in the film during its rise. Chapters four and five take up some of the important ways in which film and literature are actually alike, and chapter six tries to suggest something of the impact of the film upon modern literature. The final three chapters are concerned largely with poetry and film and with the argument that these two forms have, between them, high significance for us. For modern poetry and the film have been powerfully concerned with the problem of how to live, and how to find a humane, noncoercive order in life. Much of what is best in modern literature and in modern poetry especially comes from its constant recognition of the need for humane order, and much of what is most attractive in the film is its steady insistence, through actual visible images, on the desirability, the necessity, and upon occasion the joy of being human. Vachel Lindsay once described his book *The Art of the Moving Pictures* as a "struggle against the non-humanness of the undisciplined photograph." I should like to enroll this effort in the same struggle, and I hope further that it may be taken as a step in the direction of what George Steiner calls humane literacy.

1 / Literature and Film

HENRY ADAMS' GIFT FOR SYMBOLIC HISTORY LED him, in a famous chapter of the *Education,* to make a stylized comparison between the powerful and calm unity of the Middle Ages, and the energetic but chaotic diversity of modern times. The central symbol of the Middle Ages was for Adams the Virgin, and the concrete shape of medieval aspiration was the cathedral, particularly that of Chartres. What Adams admired in this cathedral was the visible order and harmony with which aspiration had been wrought into achievement. Singling out the southern or older tower in particular, Adams quotes Viollet-le-duc: "There is no need to dwell upon the beauty and the grandeur of composition in which the artist has given proof of rare sobriety, where all the effects are obtained, not by ornaments, but by the just and skilful proportion of the different parts. The transition, so hard to adjust, between the square base and the octagon of the *flèche,* is managed and carried out with an address which has not been surpassed in similar monuments." Adams demurs at the notion of *adresse* or cleverness, finding the tower nobler and simpler than such a word might suggest. He then quotes again, with fuller approval, from that same source. "If one tries to appreciate the conception of this tower, one will see that it is as frank as the execution is simple and skilful. Starting from the bottom, one reaches the summit of the *flèche* without marked break; without anything to interrupt the general form of the building. This *clocher*, whose base is broad, massive, and free from ornament, transforms itself, as it springs, into a sharp spire with eight faces, without its being possible to say where the massive construction ends and the light construction begins."[1]

Here as in other parts of the cathedral of Chartres, what Adams returns to again and again is the self-assured and anonymous intelligence that can produce unity without uniformity. And when Adams turns to the modern world, he finds no such force. Instead, his own times seemed to him aptly characterized by the dynamo—the electric generator, a whirling, iron, steam-driven machine using energy to produce more energy for a world in which diversity was rapidly accelerating toward chaos.

Since Adams' time it has become commonplace to remark on the chaos of modern life, the disorders apparent in everything from politics to art, and it has become easier, in this cold climate of opinion, to speak of decline than to look for new varieties of achievement. But Adams was at last pointing in a useful direction when he noted that the energy that once sought expression in the cathedral was, in his own day, expressing itself in machines. Kenneth Clark, writing in 1963, has made the point even more clearly.

> I think it is also true that human beings can produce, in a given epoch, only a certain amount of creative energy, and that this is directed to different ends and different times—music in the eighteenth century is the obvious example; and I believe that the dazzling achievements of science during the last seventy years have deflected far more of those skills and endowments which go to the making of a work of art than is usually realised. To begin with, there is the sheer energy. In every moulding of a Renaissance palace we are conscious of an immense intellectual energy, and it is the absence of this energy in the nineteenth-century copies of Renaissance buildings which makes them seem so dead. To find a form with the same vitality as a window moulding of the Palazzo Farnese I must wait till I get back into an aeroplane, and look at the relation of the engine to the wing.[2]

If Henry Adams and Kenneth Clark are right, and if science and technology have become the forms for much of the creative energy of the twentieth century, then we should not be surprised to find the motion picture, that child of the machine, of the physics of light, and of the chemistry of film, one of the most vital if indeed not the most vital of the modern arts.

The movies' roots in the late nineteenth and very early twentieth centuries are of considerable importance if one wishes to make out either the nature or the significance of this remarkable new medium. The forces of society and technology in the latter part of the nineteenth century were visibly making the world faster, stronger, and perhaps uglier. One result, predictable in retrospect, was the archly weary and exuberantly bored movement which emphasized art for the sake of itself, and translated "end of the century" into French for tone. Artiness, and the essentially decorative temperament so well epitomized in Aubrey Beardsley, had been preceded in both England and America by a genteel tradition in the arts, a tradition which quite clearly was in retreat from the big, busy, increasingly urban and industrial society. In one sense, then, the advent of the machine, or, if one accepts Henry Adams' iconography, the dynamo, had the effect of driving artists into a pose of increasing and aggressive irrelevance.

But the art for art's sake movement was not to remain the only response to the age of the dynamo. Along with a rebirth of drama in northern Europe and a revolution in poetry in England and America during the second decade of the twentieth century, the advent of the movies was due to an impulse generated from within the *fin de siècle* years. The movies are, as has been observed, a machine art for a machine age. Arnold Hauser, in the final section of his study of *The Social History of Art*, refers to the modern period as "The Film Age," and he notes that "the film is moreover, an art evolved from the spiritual foundations of technics and, therefore, all the more in accordance with the problems in store for it. The machine is its origin, its medium and its most suitable subject."[3] Film's dependence on machinery, laboratories, electricity, and modern marketing methods is of course obvious, and it seems reasonable to further claim that the film is in fact one of the great positive responses of the arts to the challenge of the dynamo.

But it is not really remarkable to find a machine age producing a machine art; if it were indeed that simple, it would have little interest other than that which attaches to routine responses to innovation. In a much subtler way, the film, itself a machine art, developed rapidly into a highly articulate critic of mechanical living. In film after film, from the earliest work of Georges Méliès, the French conjuror who turned film-maker, through the rapid rise of slapstick, the splendid Chaplin films, the cartoons, Fernand Léger's *Ballet Mécanique*, to Jacques Tati's *Mon Oncle* and beyond, the film has chronicled a vision of the inanimate world rising and taking the field against man. The motion picture has shown itself highly effective in animating the inanimate, in making the machines actors and in dramatizing the struggle between people and machines. And it is, I think, characteristic of the film in general that its portrayal of this struggle—so often written about in a weary or an angry tone which hints at defeat—was and is, in the films, an essentially comic encounter and one in which the human usually wins.

One sequence, made many times, shows a man trying to start a car. It refuses. He climbs angrily down, throws open the hood and begins to dismantle the engine, throwing the parts over his shoulder one by one; wiring, pistons, crankshaft, starter, fan, radiator, at last even the engine block. Suddenly a friend races up; he is being chased; escape is imperative. The two men quickly gather up all the engine parts, hurl them into the engine compartment and stuff down the hood. One part remains. One of the men looks at it, scratches his head, turns the part over, shrugs, pockets it. The two men leap into the car, which roars to life and races away, spilling parts all over the road.

Here too, James Agee's description of one of Buster Keaton's films is relevant. "In *Sherlock Jr.*, boiling along on the handlebars of a motorcycle quite unaware that he has lost his driver, Keaton whips through city traffic, breaks up a tug-of-war, gets a shovelful of dirt from each of a long line of Rockette-timed ditch-diggers, approaches a log at high speed which is hinged open by dynamite precisely soon enough to let him through and, hitting an obstruction, leaves the handlebars like an arrow leaving a bow, whams through the window of a shack in which the heroine is about to be violated, and hits the heavy feet-first, knocking him through the opposite wall."[4]

The variations on this theme, especially in the old silent comedies, are endless; one also recalls the wild race to the hospital at the end of *Never Give a Sucker an Even Break*, Harold Lloyd's troubles with the clock in *Safety Last*, and Chaplin's interminable struggles with even the simplest of inanimate objects. The outcome is not always happy, as witness Clouzot's *The Wages of Fear*, but in general, even if by accident much of the time, the movies insist that men usually win out when the machines rebel.

Such a response is typical of the films because, for better or worse, the films have been the most optimistic of twentieth century expressions and at the same time have remained the most thoroughly human. The flight from the human image has been most marked in painting and sculpture; this is due in part, but only in part, to the artist's disgust with a human nature that does nothing but make war with increasing viciousness. Perception of this condition leads, at times, to sculpture which is designed to resemble wreckage and painting which aims at the appearance of ruin. Literature has not often gone this far, though the steady presence of a Robinson Jeffers, a Robbe-Grillet, or a William Burroughs suggests something more than just a passing flirtation with a literature of the inhuman. The film has not been immune to abstraction, as witness much cartoon work, much experimental film, and such phenomena as the Bach sequence in *Fantasia* or *Last Year at Marienbad*, but the history of the film makes it at least arguable that the movies have, by choice rather than necessity or limitation, remained committed to the image of man to a greater degree than the other arts. In one sense, this is fit and just; the art born from the machine age becomes the art that is best fitted to assert the dignity of man just when men feel most threatened by the nervous, rapid, dissociative, and centrifugal pressures of the machine age. Born from and totally involved with the material and technical complexities so often cursed as the horror of modern life, the film has been—whether from chance or from some inherent quality is not clear—a great force for community, human values, and a visible humanity.

It has often been remarked that before the advent of the talkies, the silent film had evolved the first generally accepted universal language. Even more interesting, when one bears in mind Henry Adams' reluctant chronicle of the now lost and scattered power that once built, anonymously, the great cathedral at Chartres, is the image used by Ingmar Bergman when trying to explain why he makes films.

> There is an old story of how the cathedral of Chartres was struck by lightning and burned to the ground. Then thousands of people came from all points of the compass, like a giant procession of ants, and together they began to rebuild the cathedral on its old site. They worked until the building was completed—master builders, artists, laborers, clowns, noblemen, priests, burghers. But they all remained anonymous, and no one knows to this day who built the cathedral of Chartres.
>
> Regardless of my own beliefs and my own doubts, which are unimportant in this connection, it is my opinion that art lost its basic creative drive the moment it was separated from worship. It severed an umbilical cord and now lives its own sterile life, generating and degenerating itself. In former days the artist remained unknown and his work was to the glory of God. He lived and died without being more or less important than other artisans; "eternal values," "immortality" and "masterpiece" were terms not applicable in his case. The ability to create was a gift. In such a world flourished invulnerable assurance and natural humility.
>
> Today the individual has become the highest form and the greatest bane of artistic creation. The smallest wound or pain of the ego is examined under a microscope as if it were of eternal importance. The artist considers his isolation, his subjectivity, his individualism almost holy. Thus we finally gather in one large pen, where we stand and bleat about our loneliness without listening to each other and without realizing that we are smothering each other to death. The individualists stare into each other's eyes and yet deny the existence of each other. We walk in circles, so limited by our own anxieties that we can no longer distinguish between true and false, between the gangster's whim and the purest ideal.
>
> Thus if I am asked what I would like the general purpose of my films to be, I would reply that I want to be one of the artists in the

cathedral on the great plain. I want to make a dragon's head, an angel, a devil—or perhaps a saint—out of stone. It does not matter which; it is the sense of satisfaction that counts. Regardless of whether I believe or not, whether I am a Christian or not, I would play my part in the collective building of the cathedral.[5]

Accustomed as we have become to outsize or superheated claims from film people (even Eisenstein once said that all art strives toward the sound color stereoscopic film), we may have to think twice before taking Bergman's statement at face value. But it is a remarkable and moving credo, and one cannot imagine it being uttered with any other modern art in mind. To quote Arnold Hauser again, "the mere fact of an artistic enterprise based on cooperation is evidence of an integrating tendency of which—if one disregards the theatre, where it is in any case more a matter of the reproduction than the production of works of art—there had really been no perfect example since the Middle Ages."[6] Erwin Panofsky, in his brilliant "Style and Medium in the Moving Pictures," has also commented on this remarkable parallel between the film and the cathedral, and insofar as such comparisons have any significance beyond the illustrative, this particular one suggests that the film, like the cathedral, is one of those rare arts which are not often perfect, which rarely represent an individual achievement, and which reflect, in broad and general ways that cannot help being impressive, the spirit of a whole age, because its appeal is at last not to the specialist, but to every man.[7]

The attempt to relate literature and film is anything but new. From the early days of the film, when "classic" novels were first done into movies to the current trend toward *cinéma écriture* or *caméra stylo*, film makers have continually been indebted to literature in a wide variety of ways. So, too, a number of writers, from Pirandello to Nathanael West, have shown that the influence goes both ways. In an essay called "Dickens, Griffith, and the Film Today," Sergei Eisenstein has tried to document the importance of the English novelist to the early American film maker, and he goes on to suggest an even broader connection between film and literature. Eisenstein derides the idea that the film is an autonomous, self-contained, and utterly independent form.

> It is only very thoughtless and presumptuous people [he writes] who can erect laws and an esthetic for cinema, proceeding from premises of some incredible virgin-birth of this art!
>
> Let Dickens and the whole ancestral array, going back as far as the Greeks and Shakespeare, be superfluous reminders that both Griffith and our cinema prove our origins to be not solely as of Edison and his fellow inventors, but as based on an enormous cultured past; each part of this past in its own moment of world history has moved forward the great art of cinematography. Let this past be a reproach to those thoughtless people who have displayed arrogance in reference to literature, which has contributed so much to this apparently unprecedented art and is, in the first and most important place, the art of viewing.[8]

Eisenstein's films and his writings both show his own continued and imaginative use of literature, and it may even be urged that Eisenstein's well known "film sense" is actually an expanded version of what has been called the literary imagination.

If one considers literature as the art of words, that is to say, if it is letters or words that give literary activity its peculiar and distinctive character, then of course, we should have to say that film is obviously neither literature, nor even literary, certainly not in the silent era and only marginally or collaterally in the sound era. If it is the primacy of the word that creates or allows literature, then one would have to be content with saying that the film is at most analogous to literature, having, as it does, its own pictorial vocabulary and its montage for syntax. But if one is willing to shift the focus a little, and to describe literature as being, in the main, a narrative art, intent upon creating images and sounds in the reader's mind, then film will appear much more obviously literary itself. This description would seem to argue that the film is only an extension, but a magnificent one, of the older narrative arts.[9]

Both ideas seem to contain some truth. Film works, in its purely visual aspects, in ways that are often analogous to the ways literature works, and, considered as narrative forms, film and literature have some obvious similarities. André Bazin's *What Is Cinema?* contains some highly suggestive writing on this subject and Herbert

Read, in a general way, has described this meeting point or conjunction.

> Those people who deny that there can be any connection between the scenario and literature seem to me to have a wrong conception, so much of the film as of literature. Literature they seem to regard as something polite and academic, in other words, as something god-forsaken and superannuated, compounded of correct grammar and high-sounding ciceronian phrases. Such a conception reveals the feebleness of their sensibility. If you ask me to give you the most distinctive quality of good writing, I would give it to you in this one word: VISUAL. Reduce the art of writing to its fundamentals and you come to this single aim: to convey images by means of words. But to *convey images.* To make the mind see. To project onto that inner screen of the brain a moving picture of objects and events, events and objects moving toward a balance and reconciliation of a more than usual state of emotion with more than usual order. That is a definition of good literature—of the achievement of every good poet—from Homer and Shakespeare to James Joyce or Ernest Hemingway. It is also a definition of the ideal film.[10]

Granting that the means or mediums of film and literature are different—though perhaps not so radically different as might be supposed, as we shall see—there does seem to be enough fairly clear common ground between the two to permit the claim that the visual literacy that is still being created and enlarged by the films is an extension, or another and very closely related version, of the verbal literacy that has been associated with literature and literary culture since the Greeks.

Indeed, the currently much belabored split between the word and the image, the announcements of the end of the age of print and the advent of the age of the electronic image, and the diagnoses of post-literate man seem to me vastly to overrate the phenomena in question. The new literacy, the ability to "read" streams of visual images, has indeed, at times, the chaotic, uncontrolled, unsophisticated and exuberant qualities that often accompany a significant innovation or advance, but I think it is beginning to be apparent that this new literacy is not a negation of the older sort of literacy, but an expansion or an enlargement of the idea of literacy itself. And I suspect that the new literacy, if it takes the trouble to recognize and develop its kinship with the strictly verbal sort, will in time create a milieu for works of art that are not inferior to the best of our literary masterpieces.

It also seems arguable that the humane literacy for which George Steiner pleads so eloquently in his *Language and Silence*, and about which he is something less than sanguine, will come about, if it does come about, through some sort of union between the old and the new literacy. Mr. Steiner has spoken of the two principal functions of language as "the conveyance of humane order which we call law, and the communication of the quick of the human spirit which we call grace."[11] Film already shares the second of these functions with literature (the final scene of Fellini's *8½*, in which all the characters from the hero's life join hands to dance in a circle in a splendid gesture of assent, is one of a hundred possible examples) and film may come to share even the first of these two crucial functions.

Many people object, as Herbert Read noted, to attempts to pull the film within the realm of literature, and modern literary endeavor gives some color to this objection. For it is an odd fact, and one that is difficult to explain, that, at a time when the study of literature engages more minds, more time, and more energy than in any previous age, the scope of literary study, particularly that of the modern period, has shrunk drastically. The study of Renaissance literature used to include, and still does to a decent extent, works on theology, philosophy, education, science, history, biography, journalism, manners, morals, and navigation, in addition to poems, plays, and works of fiction. To some degree, this is true of the study of all literary periods up to the present, but the study of twentieth century literature is inexplicably confined to poems, plays, and novels, while in the universities the spread of theatre departments tends to limit the literary people more and more to just poems and fiction. This narrowing of interest to the so-called creative forms ought to favor the inclusion of dramatic films in literary study, and a recent publication by the National Council of Teachers of English called *The Motion Picture and the Teaching of English* seems to point in this direction, but it is not in this spirit that I should like to urge the study of film and literature. I should prefer a climate in which everything written, including of course film scripts, was legitimately considered a part of the study of literature, and it is in this very broad sense that I shall argue that film is a branch of literature. The claim is less sweeping than it appears, for the argument is simply that certain films and certain kinds of films are similar or related to certain works and genres of literature if we are willing to define literature broadly.

In literary studies, it is customary to regard the novel, the epic poem, the play, and a number of other genres as separate and distinct forms, each having its own qualities and strengths, its own demands and controls over its material. A good play cannot be redone as a poem, a good poem cannot be put in novel form. So too, the good dramatic film, the commonest film form, and the one that normally shows a story about people, cannot be successfully done in any other form. There has, of course, been a great deal of "adaptation" work done in the films. Countless plays and novels and even a few poems have been done into film, and a fair amount of critical attention has been paid to the connections between drama and film and novels and film. Such connections may be important, but it is necessary to realize that these connections are neither more nor less than the kind of relation usually referred to as translation, and translation, as opposed to what Dryden or Robert Lowell mean by "imitation," inevitably loses something, often much, in the process. A play may be translated into a film, but this should not obscure the fact that plays and films are not essentially similar. The Russian poet Alexander Blok understood this when he wrote in 1918, in reply to a request: "I have nothing now ready for the screen but I have more than once thought of writing for it; I always feel, however, that this will have to find a new technique for itself. In my opinion cinema has nothing in common with theatre, is not attached to it, does not compete with it, nor can they destroy each other; those once fashionable discussions 'on cinema and theatre' seem quite unreal to me. I have long loved the cinema just as it was."[12]

What is true of drama and the film is also true, most of the time, of the connection between novels and film, as George Bluestone has taken great care to show. Stories can be translated from one form to the other, but what makes a good novel rarely makes a good film. *On the Waterfront* is a good film but poor in its later novel form; Joyce's *Ulysses* is a great novel, but mediocre in its film form. Alain Resnais has put the problem straightforwardly, saying, "I would not want to shoot the adaptation of a novel because I think that the writer has completely expressed himself in the novel and that wanting to make a film of it is a little like re-heating a meal."[13]

Of the various kinds of literature, the modern novel and modern poetry come closest to the forms and methods of the dramatic film. Herbert Read has it that "the film of imagination—the film as a work of art ranking with great drama, great literature, and great painting, will not come until the poet enters the studio."[14] Others indeed claim that this has already happened and that it is still going on. Stanley Kauffmann notes that Bergman, Fellini, Antonioni "and others, including some Americans, have been extending the film into the vast areas of innermost privacy, even of the unconscious, that have been the province of the novel and of metaphysical poetry."[15] Agnes Varda has said that she wanted "to make a film exactly as one writes a novel," and Alain Resnais remarked, apropos of his *Hiroshima Mon Amour*, that he "was intending to compose a sort of poem where the image would serve only as a counterpoint to the text."[16] Jean Cocteau has made a number of films on this last principle; *Blood of a Poet* and *Orpheus* in particular are remarkable for their extensive reliance on techniques usually associated with modern poetry.

It was also Cocteau who referred to his films as studies of "the frontier incidents between one world and another."[17] The frontier he meant is that between the real and the apparent, between the actual world and the camera's world, between dreams and art, and between death and life. His description may be given another meaning, whether he intended it or not, for his films and those of a number of other gifted men are "frontier incidents" also in the sense that they take place between the world of words and the world of images.

2 /

Literary Origins and Backgrounds of the Film

SERGEI EISENSTEIN, IN HIS "DICKENS, GRIFFITH, and the Film Today," was the first to draw attention to the general importance of the novels of Charles Dickens for the early film, and he was the first to show that the work of Dickens was made relevant to the film through the innovations of D. W. Griffith. Eisenstein noted, for example, that a keen eye could have seen the close-up in the opening of *The Cricket on the Hearth* (of which Griffith made a film version) with "The kettle began it. . . ." Eisenstein also finds a similarity between Dickens' gift for bringing alive odd and minor characters, and the film's penchant for "striking figures of sympathetic old men . . . in the Dickens tradition; and these noble and slightly one-dimensional figures of sorrow, and fragile maidens; and these rural gossips and sundry odd characters." The essay notes the most famous of Griffith's borrowings from Dickens, that of cross-cutting, and Eisenstein even claims that Griffith, who is the acknowledged discoverer of montage—perhaps the most important principle in film composition—"arrived at montage through the method of parallel action, and he was led to the idea of parallel action by Dickens." Furthermore, Eisenstein suggests that Dickens' unusual visual sense led him to create the kind of characters that the film would be able to appreciate. "Perhaps the secret lies in Dickens's (as well as cinema's) creation of an extraordinary plasticity. The observation in the novels is extraordinary—as is their optical quality. The characters of Dickens are rounded with means as plastic and slightly exaggerated as are the screen heroes of today." Eisenstein notes the extent to which Dickens brought factories, machines, and railways into literature, and he goes on to note that "indication of this 'urbanism' in Dickens may be found not only in his thematic material, but also in that head-spinning tempo of changing impressions with which Dickens sketches the city in the form of a dynamic (montage) picture." Eisenstein insists that "Griffith has . . . as much a Dickens-esque sharpness and clarity as Dickens, on his part, had cinematic 'optical quality,' 'frame composition,' 'close-up,' and the alteration of emphasis by special lenses."[1]

The Russian director was well aware of the pitfalls involved in his comparative method, and the boldness of his numerous comparisons between film technique and literary technique. "Analogies and resemblances cannot be pursued too far," he noted, "they lose conviction and charm. They begin to take on the air of machination or card-tricks. I should be very sorry to lose the conviction of the affinity between Dickens and Griffith, allowing this abundance of common traits to slide into a game of anecdotal semblance of tokens."[2] Eisenstein himself rarely falls into this trap; indeed his essay makes it clear that the influence of Dickens' subjects, of his fictional techniques, and even, at times, of his tone, on the important American film innovator wedded the new film form to the older form of fictional narration. Film narration owes a debt not only to Dickens, for the film has rather extensive roots in late nineteenth century fiction.

It has been noted, for example, that film narrative, like that in the modern novel, has tended to break away from a simple, linear, temporally coherent narrative line. The film is able to break up and rearrange ordinary temporal sequence with ease; its heavy reliance on flashbacks and its preference for showing a number of things happening simultaneously give film narration a close affinity with modern Bergsonian ideas of time as something that can be manipulated.

Joseph Frank, discussing what he calls "spatial form" in modern literature, notes that this new kind of narrative goes back at least to Flaubert, and Frank cites the county fair scene in *Madame Bovary*, a scene which presents three levels of action simultaneously, as the first clear example of spatial form.[3] If the point be admitted for the modern novel, it is an easy step to claim that Flaubert's free use of time and his reliance on a visually apprehensible space shows the direction in which, and to a degree, from which, film narrative was eventually to develop.

From about the time of Henry James, the novel has become increasingly concerned with its visual qualities. James' own aim was to show the reader everything, to avoid explaining things, to avoid at all costs stepping forth and intervening, as author, in his own narrative. From this point on, the modern novel tends more and more to think of itself as something fully dramatized, the ideal being a story in which the reader *sees* everything, is *told* nothing, and in which one cannot detect the presence of the author at all. The sort of novel which, from Fielding to Thackeray and Tolstoi, had allowed the writer to discuss things—as in the essays on historiography in *War and Peace*, or Fielding's relaxed essays on a variety of topics in the opening chapter of each book of *Tom Jones*—has pretty much disappeared by the twentieth century, in favor of the fully dramatized novel. From Conrad's insistence that "my aim is to make you see" to the method of Ford Madox Ford's *The Good Soldier* and E. M. Forster's significant epigraph to *Howards End*, "Only Connect," on through most of the major fiction of the early twentieth century, the novel puts increasing emphasis on the reader's being able to "see" the entire story. And this development has had an obvious effect on the film's conception of a story. Most films follow the post-Jamesian novel in trying to present the story without the perceptible intervention of the author. Only in a few films, mostly experimental ones, has anything like the older, looser, but in some ways richer sort of novel found any reflection in the film. Cocteau's *Testament of Orpheus*, Welles' *Citizen Kane* and Fellini's *8½* seem to take steps in this direction, but the few and limited attempts serve principally to show that the main line of influence on the film narrative remains that of the main line of the modern novel.

Of some other possible influences, it is less easy to speak. Mark Twain's heavy reliance on sound, his superb ear for the vernacular, and his decision, in *Huckleberry Finn,* to use the eyes of the boy to see with may have had some indirect effects on film, once the films had acquired sound. In a way, Truffaut's *The 400 Blows* is a modern *Huckleberry Finn,* but whether Twain actually had a measurable effect on the film is not clear. It is perhaps easier to see that the emphasis on detail which characterized such literary movements as Realism and Naturalism have found expression in the films' built-in capacity for recording detail. Early films, such as Griffith's *Intolerance* or Stroheim's *Greed,* show a conscious attempt to mass detail somewhat as Zola and Dreiser had done, while Realism has had its greatest effect only recently, in the Italian Neorealist movement in the film.

In the beginning, however, the film was much less responsive to fiction than it was to drama. Béla Balázs, the Hungarian film theorist and film maker, explains this by pointing out that before the film became aware of its own distinctive methods and materials, it tended to regard itself as a means of reproducing and giving wide circulation to theatrical performances. While the film remained silent, there was, indeed, only a short road for this line of development. What good was it watching Sarah Bernhardt as Elizabeth I if one could not hear a word she said? The film's very silence forced it to turn away from theatre, except insofar as mime is theatre, but the advent of sound made filmed theatre possible again, indeed, made it fatally easy. Such recent productions as the Fonteyn-Nureyev *Romeo and Juliet,* not to mention the standard movie versions of Broadway plays from *The Front Page* to *Barefoot in the Park,* suggest that there is still some demand for the film's simple capacity to copy, for film as theatrical xerography.

While the theoretical and practical differences between film and the drama are indeed quite clear, it remains true that in some ways, other than the above, the film has inherited certain tendencies from earlier drama, and has even provided a medium that dramatists have occasionally dreamed of. There is a considerable difference between a "muse of fire" and a movie camera, but even so, the Chorus in Shakespeare's *Henry* V is a full recognition of the limitations of the stage. The Chorus comments on the fixed area available for the play, on the limited scope of action, on the need for symbolic or suggestive action, and the Chorus also recognizes the spectator's fixed point of view, and calls on the spectator's imagination to provide a sort of mobility of viewpoint. One must be careful not to over-interpret the expressed sense of theatrical limitations offered by this play, and it is greatly to the credit of Laurence Olivier's film version of *Henry* V that most of the action takes place in fixed, set-like locations provided with flattish, stagey backdrops. Olivier recognized that too much camera freedom would undercut the play as a play, and that to keep any important part of Shakespeare's intention, one would have to refrain from a full exploitation of strictly filmic techniques. The essential respect for stage drama retained by *Henry* V is not so evident in Olivier's later *Hamlet,* which may be one reason why the latter and better play is so much less effective on the screen.

But it is during the nineteenth century, when drama seemed to have exhausted its energy and to have become hopelessly moribund, that the connection between certain forms of drama and the soon to emerge film becomes most interesting. For one thing, while drama was itself languishing, theatre in the nineteenth century became more and more visually splendid, and developed toward the spectacular as it was eventually to be realized by Cecil B. DeMille. Nineteenth century spectacle culminates in the work of David Belasco, who once staged a giant Passion Play with real horses and with a one thousand watt light bulb as the King of kings.

Many good poets of the nineteenth century turned to drama in one way or another, but few of the resulting plays were much good. Not many got as far as actual production and none has had a lasting reputation. Wordsworth and Coleridge had small success with dramatic form, Wordsworth's *The Borderers* being no more distinguished than Coleridge's *Fall of Robespierre*. One of Keats' two attempts to write plays, *Otho the Great,* may be as weak as it is because it was a collaborative effort, and the other, *King Stephen,* was begun under all sort of difficulties and was never finished. Shelley's *The Cenci,* one of the few playable dramas of the time, was, even in its own time, a period piece more than anything else, its material being from Italian history and its method that of English Renaissance tragedy. Later in the century, Browning wrote a number of plays, and these, as we shall see, had an influence, again through D. W. Griffith, on the film. But in general, film owes more to closet drama of the nineteenth century than it does to actual plays, and indeed, from Byron's *Manfred* on, it seems that closet drama, or what Thomas Hardy was to call "play-shape," became a more congenial form for a number of writers than actual plays. And if closet drama lacks the power and effectiveness of great stage drama, it also lacks the limitations of the physical stage. From *Manfred* to Arnold's *Empedocles on Etna,* one can see the writer using the form of the closet drama to move the action wherever and whenever he wishes, to control point of view, and to direct our attention to great panoramas or to minute detail with complete ease and freedom.

This aspect of closet drama, its greater flexibility as regards time, place, action, and point of view, reached its extreme development in Thomas Hardy's *The Dynasts,* an epic drama on the same subject as Tolstoi's *War and Peace*. Hardy's work, in three parts, nineteen acts, and a hundred and thirty scenes, also shares with *War and Peace* an insistence on presenting the reader with an attitude toward history as well as a wealth of incident, character, and spectacle. For these two artists of the late nineteenth century, the Napoleonic wars seemed to call for a rearrangement of our ideas of history—some way to account for the astonishing and unpredictable changes that had occurred around the start of the century. As each writer tried to account for the period, and to present it fully, he found himself straining his inherited form. Tolstoi's novel is punctuated with essays on historical theory, and Hardy's immense drama has special characters (such as the Ancient Spirit of the Years), special machinery, and whole scenes devoted to dramatizing Hardy's rather fatalistic ideas about history.

Hardy seems to have chosen the dramatic form over the narrative for three main reasons: he could cover more ground moving from place to place quickly and without explanation; he could realize his theoretical ideas about history in a unique way; and most important, he could have complete freedom to explore and utilize a mobile, sensitive, rapidly shifting point of view. Hardy tried in his preface to explain the odd form of *The Dynasts:* "To say, then, in the present case, that a writing in play-shape is not to be played, is merely another way of stating that such writing has been done in a form for which there chances to be no brief definition save one already in use for works that it superficially but not entirely resembles." In retrospect, *The Dynasts* suggests that the form Hardy wanted for his Napoleonic work was quite close to what came to be known as the scenario. Hardy manipulates the point of view continually—at times it is almost as flexible as a camera on a crane—and he achieves many effects that are strikingly similar to the famous receding shot of the Confederate wounded in *Gone with the Wind.* The following is only a single example of the sort of cinematic narration to be found all through *The Dynasts.* It describes part of the action at the battle of Coruña.

> When Moore arrives at the front, Fraser and Paget move to the right, where the English are most sorely pressed. A grape-shot strikes off Baird's arm. There is a little confusion, and he is borne to the rear; while Major Napier disappears, a prisoner.
>
> Intelligence of these misfortunes is brought to Sir John Moore. He goes further forward, and precedes in person the Forty-second regiment and a battalion of the Guards who, with fixed bayonets, bore the enemy back, Moore's gestures in cheering them being notably energetic. Pursuers, pursued, and Sir John himself pass out of sight behind the hill . . . .
>
> The point of vision descends to the immediate rear of the English position. The early January evening has begun to spread its shades, and shouts of dismay are heard from behind the hill over which Moore and the advancing lines have vanished.
>
> Straggling soldiers cross in the gloom.
>
> First Straggler: He's struck by a cannon-ball, that I know; but he's not killed, that I pray God A'mighty.[4]

By 1915, when D. W. Griffith wished to do a large scale work on the American Civil War, complete with a theoretical bias and a vast scale of time and action, the result, *Birth of a Nation,* showed a striking resemblance to Hardy's *The Dynasts.*

Insofar as the two extreme and opposite developments of nineteenth century theatre, Belasco's spectacularism and the closet drama, designed exclusively to be read, have anything in common, it is a restless impatience with the limitations (and the strengths) of the legitimate stage. And both the desire to present spectacle and the wish for a form that would allow the spectator's viewpoint to change rapidly were to find their most successful expression in the new art of the film.

Among the modern forms of literature, poetry often seems to be closer to film than any other, especially in such matters of technique as the use of imagery and the use of associational logic. We have become accustomed to tracing modern poetry back to the nineteenth century; one can also trace certain elements of modern film style to the same sources. Walt Whitman's remarkable achievement, for example, has had at least as great an impact on film form as it has had on modern poetic practice. For reasons that are still debated, Whitman broke away from the standard verse forms of his time. An early poem of his, written before this break, goes in part as follows:

O, God of Columbia! O, Shield of the Free!
More grateful to you than the fanes of old story,
Must the blood-bedewed soil, the red battle-ground, be
Where our fore-fathers championed America's glory!

This is not very good by any standard; it is too bouncy and its unabashed patriotism seems rather naked in the simple metrical setting. A few years later, Whitman was to try a similar subject, but in a wholly different way:

Suddenly, out of its stale and drowsy lair, the lair of slaves,
Like lightning Europe le'pt forth,
Sombre, superb and terrible,
As Ahimoth, brother of death.

God, 'twas delicious!
That brief, tight, glorious grip
Upon the throats of kings.

The lines are irregular, but they seem reluctantly so; however, the increase in speed, energy, and vividness is obvious. These lines were to be reworked, to appear in *Leaves of Grass*. By then they had reached what is recognizable as the fully developed Whitman style:

Suddenly out of its stale and drowsy lair, the lair of slaves,
Like lightning Europe le'pt forth . . . half startled at itself,
Its feet upon the ashes and the rags . . . Its hands tight to the throats of Kings.[5]

Whitman has abandoned the metrical foot as the basic unit, and therefore, he has dropped the fixed length line. His unit is now the variable length line, carefully balanced and accented within itself to make it a rhetorical unit. He has also managed to produce a kind of verse in which a steady and consistent syntax, based on the sentence, no longer carries the meaning of the poem; this is done now by means of various sorts of parallelism, a technique to be found in old Hebrew poetry. The importance of these changes is hard to overestimate. By using the variable length line as his unit, Whitman was removing from his verse the fixed, symmetrical, and above all, orderly qualities that have marked most of Western poetry. In place of this orderliness, he put energy and excitement. His poetry gives one a sense of discovery, not a sense of pattern fulfillment. It has been argued that Whitman did this deliberately, as part of a "democratic aesthetic," associating the old world with class structure, fixed patterns of life, and rigid codes of conduct. Whitman could have felt that regular verse was a perfect vehicle for a regularized people. But America was free, growing, not fixed, not regular, and it needed, as Emerson had said, not meter but meter making argument. But whatever the reason, the new free form Whitman evolved has had a continuous influence on both poetry and, more recently, on film, and the characteristic of the Whitman line, whether one finds it in Ezra Pound, William Carlos Williams, Lawrence Ferlinghetti, D. W.

Griffith, Pare Lorentz, or Adolfas Mekas is to emphasize something other than order.

As Whitman used them, the endless varieties of parallel statement take the place of logic in developing a point. As montage was later to work in film, so Whitman used a technique of simply aligning images in such a way as to create a logic of images themselves. For example, the following from *Leaves of Grass* makes a statement about life, running from cradle to grave, but it makes the statement entirely in images:

The little one sleeps in its cradle,
I lift the gauze and look a long time, and silently brush away flies with my hand.
The youngster and the redfaced girl turn aside up the bushy hill,
I peeringly view them from the top.
The suicide sprawls on the bloody floor of the bedroom,
It is so . . . . I witnessed the corpse . . . . there the pistol had fallen.

Along with the free line and the parallelism or montage method of exposition, and related to those techniques, is Whitman's gift, or perhaps preference, for the particular. Wary of the general and the abstract, Whitman filled his poetry with long catalogues of particular things, people, and places, in much the manner in which any good documentary film builds itself up from details:

The pure contralto sings in the organloft,
The carpenter dresses his plank . . . . the tongue of his foreplane whistles its wild ascending lisp,
The married and unmarried children ride home to their thanksgiving dinner,
The pilot seizes the king-pin, he heaves down with a strong arm,
The mate stands braced in the whaleboat, lance and harpoon are ready . . .

It is notorious that while one can isolate and even define many of Whitman's techniques, it is virtually impossible to imitate Whitman's poetry. This may be partly due to the fact that what holds Whitman's techniques together, what informs and drives them, is a concept of poetry as celebration, as he himself announced in the opening line of the first poem in the first edition of *Leaves of Grass.*

> *I celebrate myself,*
> *And what I assume you shall assume,*
> *For every atom belonging to me as good belongs to you.*[6]

Celebration, as Whitman seems to have thought of it and used it, suggests that the poet is not a maker who constructs things, not a seer set apart who reveals his vision to us, not an arguer, a polemicist, or a teacher. He is simply one who bears witness to things, and his habitual set of mind is acceptance. Most of Whitman's followers have not shared his idea of poetry as celebration, or his wide and embracive habit of mind, which may help explain why they cannot control the techniques as he did. But the present point is the remarkable similarity between Whitman's poetry and the yet to be invented film. Both are conceived as widely popular; Whitman once said that "the proof of a poet is that his country absorbs him as affectionately as he has absorbed it."[7] Both evolved in America, perhaps on principles which, like Whitman's democratic aesthetic, have some origin in social and political ideas; both tend to accept and present what is before them; each is impressed, almost overawed, by the multitude and magnitude of possible subjects; both share an essentially irregular but highly energetic basic unit; and each puts a heavier reliance on juxtaposition and parallelism than on traditional syntax.

Nor is this quite all. For the tendency toward pictorial poetry that reached its peak with the Imagists, and which also had an effect on the film, can be traced to Whitman, among others. In many of his short poems, as in his longer ones, Whitman's intense visual awareness of things is insisted upon. Long catalogues mark the longer poems, while in the short ones, there may indeed be nothing more to the poem than a single image. The following poem from *Drum Taps* is, for example, only a word picture:

> *A line in long array where they wind betwixt green islands,*
> *They take a serpentine course, their arms flash in the sun—hark to*
> *the musical clank,*

Behold the silvery river, in it the splashing horses loitering stop to drink,
Behold the brown-faced men, each group, each person a picture, the negligent rest on the saddles,
Some emerge on the opposite bank, others are just entering the ford —while,
Scarlet and blue and snowy white,
The guidon flags flutter gaily in the wind.[8]

It is worth noting that such a poem seems more ordered, somehow less exhuberant, and more fixed than most of Whitman's longer poems. But the order is a visual one, a painter's kind of order of arrangement, involving strict economy of words and careful visual control of the scene. Like much film work, the poem insists only that we see the picture; the poem does not insist on a meaning.

Increasingly in the late nineteenth century, poetry that had a clear prose meaning became suspect; experience, especially inner and ecstatic experience, was undeniably richer and more interesting than the rational framework of ideas and attitudes that undertook to explain things. So Rimbaud, in "Le Bateau Ivre," could construct a vivid and terrifying collage of images which might indeed be meant as images of a state of mind, but which could not exactly be explained:

Comme je descendais des Fleuves impassibles,
Je ne me sentis plus guidé par les haleurs;
Des Peaux-Rouges criards les avaient pris pour cibles,
Les ayant cloués nus aux poteaux de couleurs.

J'étais insoucieux de tous les équipages,
Porteur de blés flamands ou de cotons anglais.
Quand avec mes haleurs ont fini ces tapages,
Les Fleuves m'ont laissé descendre ou je voulais.[9]

There was nothing perhaps so new about such an attempt. One could cite Coleridge's "Christabel," Shakespeare's songs, certain medieval lyrics, and so forth, but the deliberate attempt to go beyond the ordinary, acceptable, and orderly experience of most people became a major force in literature, as poets and others went deliberately about "exploring and colonizing inwardness," to use Erich Heller's phrase. In the Rimbaud poem, the impulse is toward discovery, as the framework is a voyage, and the method, which becomes increasingly used in modern verse, is to construct sequences of images meant to stand without explanation. Such poetry, like that of Whitman, should be called celebrational, since it is far more interested in declaring what it finds than in accounting for it. And in this sense, both modern poetry and film have become, in large part, celebrational. If Whitman's poetry has a great deal in common with a great many films from Griffith's *Intolerance* to Pare Lorentz' *The River* to Adolfas Mekas' *Hallelujah the Hills*, Rimbaud's particular approach has been taken in film by Jean Cocteau and a host of modern experimental film makers.

More conventional poets of the late nineteenth century also have had a perceptible effect on the film. Robert Browning's dramatic monologues show quite clearly his fascination with oblique angles of vision and commonly overlooked detail, while the effective and famous irony in these monologues comes from Browning's superb control over a technique which conveys, through only a single speaker, a gradually widening awareness of the disparity between what is said and what is going on. Browning's method, if I may use a metaphor from film, is to rely heavily on the sound track. He builds up a scene with a series of pictures, but the monologue is always somehow ahead of the picture, slyly undercutting it or showing it from a weak or unguarded point of view. Thus the sound does not duplicate the picture, it counterpoints it, complements it, reinterprets it, and all this interconnection gives depth and richness of texture. Browning's technique was instrumental in T. S. Eliot's poetic development, and the latter's "The Love Song of J. Alfred Prufrock" uses the same technique of interlacing sight and sound, and achieves much the same effect as Browning's better monologues. And Browning's concern to use sound to complement, rather than accompany or merely duplicate, sight emerges also in the sound motion picture as soon as directors realized that the sound, say, of a door closing, need not be accompanied by a picture of a door closing. Much of the comic effect of a film such as *Kind Hearts and Coronets* comes from the playful pictorial comments which dance along above the sober, ambitious monologues of the hero.

Gerard Manley Hopkins, another poet writing in the late nineteenth century, though his work was not published until 1918, was also revitalizing the language of poetry in ways that have interesting analogies for film. The lithe energetic freshness of Hopkins' verse bears constant witness to his strong concrete vision. His letters, his drawings, and such ideas as that of "inscape," as well as the poetry itself, all insist on a world that is full of clear, significant, and exciting detail. The poetic means by which the brilliant Jesuit poet realized this vision include a supple reworking of the syntax of English —a reworking which seemed intended to take the tiredness out of the language—and his special vocabulary, composed of old, often Anglo-Saxon words, give his poems an exciting verbal heft, a muscular sense of language with thew and sinew.

Both Hopkins' strong concrete vision of the world and his technique for energizing vocabulary and speeding up syntax were and are the sort of concern that can be realized in film as well as in poetry. As Hopkins looked at everything as though it were special, unique, and beyond price or praise, so a film like Agnes Varda's *Cleo From 5 to 7*, which is packed with lovingly photographed bits of Paris, leaves one with the feeling that the director has fully seen and fully acknowledged the separate existence of every stone, tree, window, step, and bench in its own right. Her film, like Hopkins' poetry, is a way of praising the world. Such work leaves one oddly elated, a little more aware of the form and life of things, eager to see the world more fully oneself. And Hopkins' vocabulary, selected for its heft or muscle, and his rippling, somehow freer syntax is very much like the editing in Truffaut's or Lelouch's films.

Yeats once edited an anthology of modern verse, and for the opening selection, he went to Walter Pater's now famous description of the Mona Lisa and wrote it out as free verse. Pater's original, while it is only prose, is however quite similar to both film and modern free verse.

> She is older than the rocks among which she sits; like the vampire, she has been dead many times, and learned the secrets of the grave; and has been a diver in deep seas, and keeps their fallen day about her; and trafficked for strange webs with Eastern merchants, and, as Leda, was the mother of Helen of Troy, and as Saint Anne, the mother of Mary; and all this has been to her but as the sound of lyres and flutes, and lives only in the delicacy with which it has moulded the changing lineaments, and tinged the eyelids and the hands.[10]

Among other things, this is an example of what Yeats called "object without contour," a characteristic not only of modern painting and poetry, but of the film as well. What Pater has done with La Gioconda, Antonioni has done with Monica Vitti and Fellini with Giulietta Massina. It is perhaps even more significant that a poet like Yeats should trace modern poetry back to this prose description of a painting that is done in such a way as to be acceptable as poetry as well. The passage, foreshadowing the now blurred distinction between prose and poetry—a distinction less important now than matters of tone, image, and syntax—suggests the possibility of drawing from or working with several of the arts at once, and relies heavily on simply replacing one image with another without stopping to explain just how the two are related, a technique widely used in both film and modern poetry.

If the tenuous connections glanced at above are only perceptible to the less than disinterested vision of hindsight, the actual connection between modern poetry and the film may be shown to have started between 1910 and 1920. Several concerns and discoveries which influenced the poetic movement known as Imagism had a modest but contemporaneously acknowledged effect on the movies. One of these concerns was a fascination with hieroglyphics which Pound, following Fenollosa, did much to spread. Ernest Fenollosa, the great oriental scholar, pointed out that the Chinese language constructed words pictorially. An idea is acted out in an elaborate form of picture writing called an ideogram. Much of the freshness of early twentieth century poetry must owe something to Pound's wide-eyed endorsement of Fenollosa's observation. Who could not see that pictorial symbols which showed the sun underlying the bursting forth of plants were more alive, more vivid than abstractions like "spring"? So impressed was Fenollosa with the communicative possibilities of a language of pictures with only arrangement in space for syntax, that he challenged the whole idea of the sentence. He protested that the form or structure of the sentence—essentially subject-object-verb—adds little if anything to the verbal unit from which it builds. Pound thought Fenollosa's work sufficiently interesting to call it "a study of the fundamentals of all aesthetics."[11]

With or without a taste for superlatives and a willingness to ignore or dismiss the function of prose, we must consider it more than an accident that the poetry of the advance guard was discovering and exploiting the ability of words to form pictures and the idea of connecting words by juxtaposition rather than with conventional syntax at the same time that the film was doing just that itself. There is, for example, a remarkable similarity between Pound's own "In a Station of the Metro," which consists only of the two lines "The apparition of these faces in the crowd/Petals on a wet, black bough," and the film sequence of Eisenstein which shows first a crowd slowly beginning to stir with anger, followed at once by a shot of the ice on a river breaking up tumultuously. In each case, two pictures are simply joined together or juxtaposed to form a unit. Neither unit has a verb at all. Pound does not say whether the crowd is like or unlike the flowers or whether the crowd reminds him of flowers, moves like flowers, is as temporary as flowers, or what. All we have is the juxtaposition, which says without specifying, that the two images are related. Pound's poem, like many others of the time, is poetry as a visual art. Or one might say that Eisenstein's sequence is film using the techniques of poetic imagism.

Vachel Lindsay noticed the similarity, or more exactly, the applicability of some of the ideas of the Imagists, among whom he listed Pound, Richard Aldington, John Gould Fletcher, Amy Lowell, F. S. Flint, and D. H. Lawrence, to the film. What Lindsay noted was the capacity of both Imagist poetry and the film—then silent, of course—for working with "space measured without sound plus time measured without sound." Realizing what was undeniably true at the time, that the writers were better disciplined and more craftsmanlike than the film makers, Lindsay proposed that followers of the Imagists should seek expression in film.

Lindsay also wrote a suggestive chapter on the resemblance between the Egyptian hieroglyphic alphabet and the modern development of a visual alphabet in the film. "The invention of the photoplay is as great a step as was the beginning of picture-writing in the stone age. And the cave-men and women of our slums seem to be the people most affected by this novelty, which is but an expression of the old in that spiral of life which is going higher while seeming to repeat the ancient phase." While Lindsay did not go so deeply as Fenollosa into the possible implications of the new syntax required by picture language, he did remark on the previously undistinguished record of the English and Americans in the visual arts. Pointing out that literary traditions were stronger, older, and more self-sustaining in England and America than the few bursts of achievement in sculpture, painting, and architecture, Lindsay saw the film as an important educative form for us. "A tribe," he wrote, "that has thought in words since the days that it worshipped Thor and told legends of the cunning of the tongue of Loki, suddenly begins to think in pictures."[12] Lindsay's comment may help explain why, in England and America at least, it took so long for the film to begin to aspire to a level of achievement comparable to that of contemporaneous literature.

Still, meagre as the above hints and notes may be, it seems clear that by 1915 or so, the film had begun to be aware that it was more than a toy or a novelty and had commenced to reach for and rather noisily claim status as a genuine art. What was happening, both in practice, in the films of Griffith, and in theory, such as Lindsay's *The Art of the Moving Picture*, was that the film was beginning to discover and adopt concerns, techniques, approaches, and material that had once been exclusively literary. But both the new literature and the rising film were responding to new challenges and pressures, reforms and renewals, that had roots in the late nineteenth century and were becoming increasingly insistent during the first two decades of the twentieth century. The film arrived as a new answer to certain literary searches, such as Hardy's for a mobile point of view, or the Imagists' concern with vividness and picturization. Thus by 1920 or so, film and literature were rather firmly linked, though this was not particularly clear at the time, by a common heritage and by certain similarities of technique, approach, and even subject matter.

3 /

Griffith and Eisenstein: The Uses of Literature in Film

FROM THE DAY IN 1896 WHEN THE LUMIÈRE brothers first exhibited their new device and showed to delighted and terrified audiences the spectacle of a railroad engine rushing up toward them, it was apparent that things and people in motion were the natural subject matter for the new medium. Accordingly, Vachel Lindsay, writing in 1915, divided films into what he called "pictures of intimacy" or "painting in motion," "pictures of action" or "sculpture in motion," and "pictures of spectacle" or "architecture in motion." What was less apparent in the early days of the film was just how the new medium was actually to treat its subject matter. It was not at first clear that film had any real principles that belonged to it and to no other form. But film historians are now pretty generally agreed that the development of the film's peculiar form is to be found in the progression from Georges Méliès to Edwin S. Porter to D. W. Griffith and Sergei Eisenstein. And the common thread of this development is the discovery and application of the film's narrative capacities.

Méliès, a magician before he came to the movies, saw at once the possibilities in film for illusion. His work, done mostly at the turn of the century, is full of trick shots, flying bodies, expanding heads, and so on. Méliès was the first to be conscious that the film could do more than reproduce reality, that it could in fact rearrange reality at will. (Indeed, as Rudolf Arnheim has carefully shown, the photographed image is not at all a simple representation of reality, because of the many inherent distortions involved in producing an image by photography, such as the alteration of depth perception, flattening of planes, relative distances, and sizes, etc.)[1] Méliès had no very sophisticated knowledge of just how the camera changes the reality it photographs, but his perception that the film could treat reality in odd or "magical" ways meant that henceforward the process of filming could be regarded as more than a procedure for passive recording; it could be used in a positive or active fashion to interpret or select. What is significant about Méliès's work is that, for the first time, someone regarded the film as a medium, and the machinery as only machinery, both to be utilized by the man behind the camera in such a way as to impose his own vision upon his material. Méliès's step, simple and insignificant as it now seems, and trivial as his films are, made the first and necessary effort to give the film maker a self-conscious sense that he could in fact control what the spectator would see.

The Great Train Robbery, made in 1903 by the American Edwin S. Porter, took the next step, also very simple but very important. Up to Porter's time, the custom was to act out a story in front of the camera, the action being continuous and in one place, the camera remaining fixed and immovable like a spectator in a theatre. Porter's story took place in more than one location, and, as a result, he had to splice the scenes together in order to tell the story. What he had invented was editing and cutting, and what he had given the film, though it was years before it was fully recognized, was the beginning of the basic language of the film. Each shot is like a word. Literature makes sense and significance of words by joining them together. So in the movies, it is the cutting, joining, editing, or in its most elaborate form, montage, that provides the grammar and syntax of film.

The contributions of Méliès and Porter seem to have been largely owing to luck or accident, for nothing much came of them until David Wark Griffith began to make films. Not a great artist, Griffith had, however, an incalculable influence on the development of the movies: *Birth of a Nation* (1915) was the first real indication that the movies had "arrived" in America; *Intolerance*—shown in Russia in 1919—may be said to have startled that nation into an awareness of the new medium's potential. It was as a technician that Griffith elaborated, in a clear and purposeful way, the essential language of film. Griffith had a literary and theatrical background, and the idea of using the camera to interpret rather than to merely record seems to have come naturally. Béla Balázs, whose *Theory of the Film* is perhaps the best single book on film yet written, flatly says that the art of the film was born in America in the work of Griffith, and Balázs thus summarizes the principles that Griffith first used:

1. Varying distance between spectator and scene within one and the same scene; hence varying dimensions of scenes that can be accommodated within the frame and composition of a picture.
2. Division of the integral picture of the scene into sections, or 'shots.'
3. Changing angle, perspective and focus of 'shots' within one and the same scene.
4. Montage, that is the assembly of 'shots' in a certain order in which not only whole scene follows whole scene (however short) but pictures of smallest details are given, so that the whole scene is composed of a mosaic of frames aligned as it were in chronological sequence.[2]

What Griffith had done was to separate film from theatre, for in the beginning, film, like theatre, presented a flowing tableau in a fixed space to a spectator (the camera and, of course, the viewer) who was also set in a fixed place. Griffith gave the camera mobility, and in so doing, he hit upon the peculiar form henceforth called, rather jarringly, filmic. A film was to be composed of all sorts of shots taken from all sorts of angles and distances. What gave the finished film coherence was not, as in theatre, consecutive action in a fixed locale, but a logic or continuity created by the sequences into which the shots were joined together. Some time later the Russian film maker Pudovkin tried, at the start of a book on film technique, to sum up this most fundamental way in which film works by means of an analogy with literature. "To the poet or writer separate words are as raw material. They have the widest and most variable meanings which only begin to become precise through their position in the sentence. To that extent to which the word is an integral part of the composed phrase, to that extent is its effect and meaning variable until it is fixed in position, in the arranged artistic form. . . . To the film director each shot of the finished film subserves the same purpose as the word to the poet."[3]

Griffith's influence on the film was decisive, and it is thus of considerable importance that we should be aware of the extent to which Griffith's literary knowledge and preoccupations found expression in his film work. Griffith's first ambition had been to become a writer, and it was only gradually and with reluctance that he gave it up. He had had one play produced before he turned to the films—initially as an actor—and all through his early years as a film maker, he was so ashamed of his disgraceful employment that he refused to use his real name.[4] To his initial literary vocation, we must add, as Lewis Jacobs has noted, in his excellent chapters on Griffith in *The Rise of the American Film,* the love of Victorian literature, particularly poetry, which can be seen both in Griffith's early subjects and in his style. He admired Browning, Kingsley, Tennyson, and Hood, and during his first year as a movie director he adapted works by Jack London, Tennyson, Shakespeare, Hood, Tolstoi, Poe, O. Henry, Reade, Maupassant, Stevenson, and Browning for the screen. Despite his theatrical background, it was not exclusively drama, as the above list shows, that influenced his films. When, for example, Griffith was asked where he got the idea for cross-cutting, that is, jumping back and forth between parallel stories or parallel parts of one story, he replied, according to legend, that that was the way Dickens wrote novels. Of course the technique of keeping more than one narrative line going in a single work had not been new with Dickens (one can see it for example in the English Renaissance drama) but the fact that Griffith picked it up from Dickens shows his awareness of the usefulness of literature other than drama for the film.

Griffith was also fascinated by the work and even the personality of Edgar Allan Poe. In 1909, his first year as a director, Griffith made a film called *Edgar Allan Poe*, which romantically dramatized some of the legends about Poe's unhappy life, and later Griffith directed a film called *The Avenging Conscience*, which pulled material from "The Telltale Heart," "Annabel Lee," "The Black Cat," and "William Wilson." Griffith was attracted by Poe's theme of conscience and by the dark visions into which Poe wove the theme, but Griffith seems also to have picked up some of Poe's genius for rhythm, pace, and timing. Poe's better stories, like Griffith's better films, work on the principle of acceleration. Beginning slowly, the narrative gradually quickens, the focus narrows, the action speeds up, is pushed to a climax, and then abruptly halted. Griffith was the first film maker to discover that slow editing (shots which remain on the screen a long time, even if they are shots of violent and rapid action) will automatically slow the pace, while fast editing (the use of short shots, even if of static material) will quicken and speed the rhythm of the film. It is possible that Griffith's use of such devices came partly from his careful reading and filmic reworking of Poe's work.

Another literary figure to whom Griffith turned was Walt Whitman. Whitman's potential connection with the film had already been noted by Vachel Lindsay, who wrote: "We must have Whitmanesque scenarios, based on moods akin to that of the poem *By Blue Ontario's Shore*. The possibility of showing the entire American population its own face in the Mirror Screen has at last come. Whitman brought the idea of democracy to our sophisticated literati, but did not persuade the democracy itself to read his democratic poems. Sooner or later the kinetoscope will do what he could not, bring the nobler side of the equality idea to the people who are so crassly equal."[5] Griffith did not fulfill these hopes, perhaps no one really has, but the young American director did try. For *Intolerance*, a film composed of four stories, widely separate in space and time, Griffith borrowed Whitman's technique of the ruling image.[6] "Song of Myself" exfoliates and spreads around the image of the grass, repeated over and over in different ways. For *Intolerance* Griffith lifted the cradle endlessly rocking from Whitman's poem of that name. Griffith rather crudely overdid it, however, as he simply photographed Lilian Gish rocking a cradle, and then just repeated the shot, cutting it in over and over. Where Whitman's poems grow from and around a central image or group of images, Griffith simply tried to impose a central symbol on his sprawling and previously conceived material. He is thus nowhere near as successful as Whitman, but the attempt alone is significant.

Wherever one looks in Griffith's early career, one will find, for better or worse, a strong literary impulse at work. *Birth of a Nation* owes much of what is good in it to Griffith's attempt to bring literary epic alive in film, and much of what is worst in it to its literary basis in Thomas Dixon's *The Clansman*. And it was while trying to make a film version of Browning's *Pippa Passes* (1909) that Griffith began to experiment with light, changing the angles, and varying the amount of light on his set. Obvious as such practice seems now, this was the beginning of the film's awareness that film making is essentially a process of painting with light, and the beginning of the realization that the control of light and shadow was one of the film's basic pictorial principles.

After Griffith, the man who did the most to shape film form as it still exists was Sergei Eisenstein. His pervasive influence on the film has been threefold. His films, from *Strike* and *Potemkin* through *Ivan the Terrible* and the unfinished Mexican film, have set standards for films that have rarely been surpassed; his influence as a teacher was wide and productive; and his writings represent the most articulate rationale of the film maker's art that has been produced by any practicing director. His writings are excited and vivid, and his influence is far from spent, as much because of his brilliant theoretical flair as for his enormous learning, wide reading, and his constant meticulous insistence upon detail.

Eisenstein did a good deal of work in theatre before turning to films, but became so out of sympathy with the nature of acted drama that he once produced a play about a gas factory in a gas factory, moving his audience from one part of the plant to another for succeeding scenes. Such a phenomenon strikes one as rather similar to the current "happenings," which also confuse, deliberately of course, art with reality, but in Eisenstein's case it seems to have been a restless search for form rather than a naive enthusiasm for realism pushed to the extent of reality. Neither his films nor his books suggest a reliance on the truth-to-life theory of film. Indeed they suggest quite the reverse, and in support of his insistent claim that the film is a medium capable of high art, Eisenstein ransacked literature for examples and lessons for the new form.

The epigraph to *The Film Sense* is a quotation from John Livingston Lowes' *The Road to Xanadu,* the famous analysis of the creative process behind Coleridge's "Kubla Khan."

> Every word has been permeated, as every image has been transmuted, through the imaginative intensity of one compelling creative act. 'Consider it well,' says Abt Vogler of the musician's analogous miracle:
>
> *Consider it well: each tone of our scale in itself is nought.*
> *It is everywhere in the world—loud, soft, and all is said:*
> *Give it to me to use! I mix it with two in my thought:*
> *And, there! Ye have heard and seen: consider and bow the head!*
>
> Give Coleridge one vivid word from an old narrative; let him mix it with two in his thought; and then (translating terms of music into terms of words) out of three sounds he [will] frame, not a fourth sound, but a star.[7]

The epigraph points to and was seen by Eisenstein as illuminating his theory of montage, and it is significant that he grounds the idea by referring to the creative process of the poet. For Eisenstein, then, the film maker relies on very much the same imaginative process as the writer, as his continuing references to literature make even more clear.

Eisenstein argues that the crucial idea of montage is the fact "that two film pieces of any kind, placed together, inevitably combine into a new concept, a new quality, arising out of that juxtaposition," and he cites parallels from literature in an effort to clarify the idea for the reader.[8] An extreme instance, he suggests, is to be found in Lewis Carroll's description of the *portmanteau* word. "For instance, take the two words 'fuming' and 'furious.' Make up your mind that you will say both words, but leave it unsettled which you will say first. Now open your mouth and speak. If your thoughts incline ever so little towards 'fuming,' you will say 'fuming-furious'; if they turn, by even a hair's breadth, toward 'furious,' you will say 'furious-fuming'; but if you have that rarest of gifts, a perfectly balanced mind, you will say 'frumious.' "[9] Eisenstein notes the obvious, that the great master of this technique is Joyce, but his point, applicable to literature as well as film, is to show that the juxtaposition of two things produces not a sum of the two things, but a new entity.

It has sometimes been assumed that film is a fatally easy form, since to see is to perceive, but Eisenstein was well aware that what is visible is not always understood. He makes the point not from film, but from Tolstoi. "When Vronsky looked at his watch on the Karenins' verandah he was so agitated and so preoccupied that he saw the hands and the face of the watch without realizing the time."[10] Elsewhere, as he discusses how to build separate representations up into a single effective image, he turns to Maupassant's description of a young man waiting for a girl; "He went out towards eleven o'clock, wandered about some time, took a cab, and had it drawn up in the Place de la Concorde, by the Ministry of Marine. From time to time he struck a match to see the time by his watch. When he saw midnight approaching, his impatience became feverish. Every moment he thrust his head out of the window to look. A distant clock struck twelve, then another nearer, then two together, then a last one, very far away. When the latter had ceased to sound, he thought; 'It is all over. It is a failure. She won't come.' "[11] What Eisenstein admired in the above is the way the emotional quality of midnight is brought home to the reader by having not one, but a series of clocks ring it out. Simpler and worse would have been a plain announcement, "the clock struck midnight." Here, as elsewhere, Eisenstein's thoughtful literary examples show him searching for ways to avoid a simple reliance on the obvious, and attempting to work for subtler and stronger effects.

Much of the initial chapter of *The Film Sense* is given to the idea that montage, the crucial principle for film in Eisenstein's eyes, actually exists in other arts as well. Eisenstein prints a description by Leonardo da Vinci for a projected but never realized painting of the Deluge, and when Eisenstein says that the description is a "virtual shooting script," he means only that Leonardo's technique, as revealed by the description, could easily be called a montage approach. The opening of this remarkable description is as follows:

> Let the dark, gloomy air be seen beaten by the rush of opposing winds wreathed in perpetual rain mingled with hail, and bearing hither and thither a vast network of the torn branches of trees mixed together with an infinite number of leaves.
>
> All round let there be seen ancient trees uprooted and torn in pieces by the fury of the winds.
>
> You should show how fragments of mountains, which have been already stripped bare by the rushing torrents, fall headlong into the very torrents and choke up the valleys,
>
> Until the pent-up rivers rise in flood and cover the wide plains and their inhabitants.
>
> Again there might be seen huddled together on the tops of many of the mountains many different sorts of animals, terrified and subdued at last to a state of tameness, in company with men and women who had fled there with their children.
>
> And the fields which were covered with water had their waves covered over in great part with tables, bedsteads, boats and various other kinds of rafts, improvised through necessity and fear of death,
>
> Upon which were men and women with their children, massed together and uttering various cries and lamentations, dismayed by the fury of the winds which were causing the waters to roll over and over in mighty hurricane, bearing with them the bodies of the drowned.[12]

The whole sequence is organized, Eisenstein notes, beginning with the heavens and returning to it at the (not quoted) end; within this frame, the humans are at the center, and the description works carefully, setting detail against background, close-up against long shot. Eisenstein notes that "in perfect clarity emerge the typical elements of a montage composition." The painting will not actually move, of course, the figures will not walk or run, but Eisenstein is interested not in mere movement, but in how selection of detail and the editorial joining of images works, and he points out that "Leonardo's exceedingly sequential description fulfills the task not of merely listing the details, but of outlining the trajectory of the future movement of the attention over the surface of the canvas. Here we see a brilliant example of how, in the apparently static simultaneous 'co-existence' of details in an immoble picture, there has yet been applied exactly the same montage selection, there is exactly the same ordered succession in the juxtaposition of details, as in those arts that include the time factor."[13]

In the perspective offered here, it becomes clear that what is called montage in the film is indeed a way of ordering material that both literature and the visual arts have always used. Further on, and descending now to details, Eisenstein cites passages from Pushkin's poetry to show how one selects and positions particular details to achieve particular effects. The actual mechanics of montage, he points out, are just as clear in Pushkin as they are in a film.

> *But no one knew just how or when*
> *She vanished. A lone fisherman*
> *In that night heard the clack of horses' hoofs,*
> *Cossack speech and a woman's whisper. . . .*[14]

Eisenstein points out that Pushkin here gives us the information that the girl, Marya, has vanished, but then by the three bits of sound—horses' hoofs, Cossack speech, and a whisper—goes on to force us to an emotional realization of the girl's vanishing. Eisenstein also quotes from the same poem, *Poltava,* a description of Peter the Great, which in its strange static intensity reminds one of Eisenstein's own *Ivan the Terrible.*

> *And then with highest exaltation*
> *There sounded, ringing, Peter's voice:*
> *"To arms, God with us!" From the tent,*
> *By crowding favorites surrounded,*
> *Peter emerges. His eyes*

Are flashing. His look is terrible.
His movements swift. Magnificent he,
In all his aspect, wrath divine.
He goes. His charger is led him.
Fiery and docile faithful steed.[15]

Such is Eisenstein's attention to the details of literary presentation that he carefully notes the importance of the inverted opening. Pushkin does not start out with Peter's words, but leads up to them. If we wanted to get a similar effect in film, Eisenstein goes on, we "must transmit it so that there is an ordered succession, revealing first its *exaltation*, then its ringing quality, followed by our *recognition of the voice* as Peter's, and finally, to distinguish *the words* that this exalted, ringing voice of Peter *utters*."[16] For the benefit of his English readers, Eisenstein also draws examples from English poetry. Shelley and Keats provide the material for his discussion of enjambment, the technique of joining lines tightly together by running the sense on over the natural line breaks. Eisenstein quotes from *Endymion:*

Thus ended he, and both
Sat silent: for the maid was very loth
To answer; feeling well that breathed words
Would all be lost, unheard, and vain as swords
Against the enchased crocodile, or leaps
Of grasshoppers against the sun. . . .[17]

He suggests that the film maker can learn from such poetry how to edit more effectively, and indeed, the above example shows a technique now standard in film, that of cutting on motion, that is to say, cutting one shot into another during, not after, some piece of motion.

A final example here of Eisenstein's patient practical study of literature will be his discussion of *Paradise Lost*. Students of Milton may raise an eyebrow at hearing the great epic described as "a first-rate school in which to study montage and audio-visual relationships," but Eisenstein makes a fascinating case for his claim. He quotes a series of passages to show that, as a rule, Milton averages one picture per line, but that the lines are so worked out that the pictures are rarely coterminous with the lines, thus providing a well knit and varied whole. For example, where the rebellious angels are cast into Hell, Milton gives the following description:

The overthrown he rais'd, and as a Heard
Of Goats or timerous flock together throngd
Drove them before him Thunder-struck, pursu'd
With terrors and with furies to the bounds
And Chrystall wall of Heav'n, which op'ning wide,
Rowld inward, and a spacious Gap disclos'd
Into the wastful Deep; the monstrous sight
Strook them with horror backward, but far worse
Urg'd them behind; headlong themselves they threw
Down from the verge of Heav'n, Eternal wrauth
Burnt after them to the bottomless pit.

Eisenstein worked the passage out as a shooting script, each numbered "shot" representing one image or picture from Milton's passage.

1. *The overthrown he rais'd, and*
2. *as a Heard of Goats or timerous flock together throngd*
3. *drove them before him Thunder-struck,*
4. *pursu'd with terrors and with furies to the bounds and Chrystall wall of Heav'n,*
5. *which op'ning wide, rowld inward,*
6. *and a spacious Gap disclos'd*
7. *into the wastful Deep;*
8. *the monstrous sight strook them with horror backward,*
9. *but far worse urg'd them behind;*
10. *headlong themselves they threw down from the verge of Heav'n*
11. *Eternal wrauth burnt after them to the bottomless pit.*

Eisenstein calls attention to the "contrapuntal design of non-coincidences between the limits of the representations and the limits of the rhythmical articulations," which seems to be a difficult way of saying that there is a calculated discrepancy between the images and the iambic pentameter lines.[18] If the relation between line structure, rhythm and sequence, and the pictorial and audible content provides an example for the film maker, it also seems to be an interesting way of approaching Milton's poetry. From the way Eisenstein approaches Milton's battle scenes, it is possible to infer that the battle scenes in *Alexander Nevsky* owe a great deal to Milton, and a detailed comparative study along the lines suggested above might serve to illuminate both works.

Thus Eisenstein does more than fall back on literature for analogy, or support, or prestige. He quite clearly advocates the careful study of literary technique as an essential prepartion for the film maker. Though his own argument rests almost completely on montage, and may require broadening, still montage is crucial in the film. Eisenstein's insistence that montage is to be found everywhere in literature (he actually claims montage to be crucial to all the arts, but his references to painting and sculpture are usually to literary descriptions of them) makes it appear that to a considerable degree Eisenstein's film sense is actually a sort of expanded literary sense expressed through the new medium of film. Whether or not one wishes to go this far, it should be evident, from the work of both Griffith and of Eisenstein, that literature has in fact had a decisive influence upon the film, both in theory and in practice. Eisenstein, in particular, makes it clear that the connection is not peripheral or figurative, but in some sense organic and crucial.

The history of the film after Eisenstein shows even further deepenings and widenings of the literary influences on the film. The advent of sound quickly reduced film to filmed theatre, but as soon as film makers learned to use sound "shots" the way they were accustomed to using visual "shots" the sound film recovered its balance, and from Eisenstein's own *Alexander Nevsky* to the recent *Sundays and Cybele* and the films of Alain Resnais and many others, the film has managed to connect the word with the image with increasing significance and sophistication.

No study of literary influences on film could ignore the fact that a great many talented writers have written for the films. The list includes Fitzgerald, Faulkner, Dylan Thomas, James Agee, Nathanael

West, Malcolm Lowry, Jean-Paul Sartre, Christopher Isherwood, John Osborn, Alain Robbe-Grillet, Marguerite Duras, and innumerable others. But with very few exceptions, these writers' actual involvement with the movies has had little real influence on film form or film style. In what must be one of the greatest miscarriages of talent ever to occur, most of the writers who wrote films went to Hollywood for money, wrote condenscendingly for the "dream factory," and never found a way to challenge or change the massive and usually puerile film industry's concept of what makes a good movie. It is true that James Agee's version of *The African Queen* set a new standard for filmed novels, but Agee's best film script, *Noa-Noa*, remains unproduced. And the screen version of Hemingway's *To Have and Have Not*, prepared by William Faulkner, shows how Hollywood could preside over a conjunction of geniuses only to produce, by a sort of cross-sterilization, a perfectly ordinary vehicle for Humphrey Bogart. The collision between Hollywood and most of the writers who have gone there has produced more good novels about and against Hollywood than it has produced decent films.

More recently, with the rise of the new French cinema, literary concerns and ideas have been increasingly emphasized by Astruc, Agnes Varda, Truffaut, Resnais, Marker, and others. France has, of course, always had directors with literary interests, both René Clair and Jean Cocteau are examples, but the new French cinema is almost aggressively literary in both its films and its pronouncements. Resnais called *Hiroshima Mon Amour* a "sort of poem," his *Night and Fog* is a fine achievement in its integration of a literary text with two visual "texts," one in black and white, the other in color, and his *Last Year at Marienbad*, made in collaboration with the novelist Robbe-Grillet, has more affinities with the modern experimental novel than it has with most films. Agnes Varda has said that she wishes "to make a film exactly as one writes a novel," and Alexandre Astruc is perhaps most explicit of all. "I call this new age that of the Caméra-Stylo. This image has a precise significance. It means that the cinema will free itself little by little from the tyranny of the visual, of the image for its own sake, of the immediate anecdote, of the concrete, to become a means of writing as supple and subtle as that of the written language."[19]

From its beginning to the present, then, film has been reaching for and appropriating to its own use ideas, forms, and devices that were once exclusively literary, or which can be expressed by means of analogies with literature. It now remains to inquire into the nature and extent of the common ground shared by literature and film, into the extent to which literature and film can and do use their obviously different media to express, create, or communicate similar kinds of experience.

4 / Literary Technique and Film Technique

Analogies between film and literature are not new; Eisenstein in particular was an adept at finding ingenious and suggestive parallels, and once one begins to look for them, they can be found everywhere. I will, therefore, limit myself here to noting some literary parallels for only a few of the film's most characteristic devices, devices sometimes treated as though there were no equivalents in other arts.

It is often noted that the film, because of its basis in photography, has a unique capacity to deal with the concrete and the visible, and to record things as they are. Such an impulse can be seen behind the final sequence of Antonioni's *Eclipse,* in which the director tries, after the story is over, to gather up the visible fragments of the world of the film into a telling image of paralysis and futility. The sequence goes in part as follows:

> The shadow of a tree against a white wall.
>
> Two shadows on the asphalt pavement, cast by the rays of a sun that is not very bright.
>
> A panoramic shot of the stadium behind which Piero and Vittoria had often strolled together and which is now vacant. The street is completely empty.

The white traffic stripes painted on the asphalt for the benefit of the pedestrians. Footsteps are heard. They are those of a passing stranger.
The wooden fence along the house under construction. The stranger disappears into the background.
The leaves of a tree trembling in the wind. . . .[1]

It is an impressive sequence, eerie, empty, yet powerful. It runs on for some five minutes on the screen, and its cumulative effect is of the eclipse of man. Its technique is not that of simple realism, but of deliberately chosen details intended to create a single general impression. It is, in short, the same technique that the writer of the book of Ecclesiastes used to make much the same point:

> Remember now thy Creator in the days of thy youth, while the evil days come not, nor the years draw nigh, when thou shalt say, I have no pleasure in them;
>
> While the sun, or the light, or the moon, or the stars, be not darkened, nor the clouds return after the rain:
>
> In the day when the keepers of the house shall tremble, and the strong men shall bow themselves, and the grinders cease because they are few, and those that look out of the windows be darkened,
>
> And the doors shall be shut in the streets.[2]

The technique these two efforts share is the careful selection and presentation of particular concrete images in order to create a single, overwhelming, and quite abstract proposition, that all is vanity or emptiness.

Ever since the filmed conjuring tricks of George Méliès, the film has been recognized as able to handle metamorphoses and "magical" changes in a special way. One scene can be made to dissolve into another; for example, a garden can go from winter to summer in a moment; a flower can blossom out in a few seconds; princes can change into beasts. The work of Jean Cocteau comes to mind at once, but the change or transformation is a common technique. The laboratories have made this process easy, perhaps too easy, for the film, since it has rarely been done with the effectiveness that Ovid, Spenser, Pound, or even Pater brought to the same device. The film is usually content to handle a metamorphosis by simply replacing one image with another, allowing the first to "dissolve" into the second. Film rarely tries to show one thing actually changing into something else. For the latter effect, we must turn to a writer such as Ovid, who gives this picture of the nymph Cyane changing into a fountain:

The queen of waters all to water went:
Before your eyes, the limbs turned soft, the bone
Bent, and the toughness of the nails was gone;
The parts most slender, fingers, legs, and feet,
And wave-hued tresses—These did soonest fleet;
Since limbs least solid, being most near allied
To the cool element, easiest liquified;
Then shoulders went; and breast and sides and back
Dissolved, and vanished into watery rack;
And when the lifeblood in the flaccid veins
Turns water, nothing tangible remains.[3]

The film is also proud, and justly so, of its capacity to present a stream of images which make a point or create an effect without logical connection or explanation. Wordless sequences of summer love, or the loneliness of a young man or woman are as common as they are effective. Yet even this montage of images is a technique that poets have long known. Modern poetry uses it extensively and it would often seem as though modern poetry had learned the technique from the film, if one could not find it at least as far back as Keats:

The calmest thoughts come round us—as of leaves
   Budding,—fruit ripening in stillness,—autumn suns
Smiling at eve upon the quiet sheaves,—
Sweet Sappho's cheek,—a sleeping infant's breath,—
   The gradual sand that through an hour-glass runs,—
A woodland rivulet,—a Poet's death.[4]

Image replaces image, there is no prose logic, no assertion. The sense of process motivates the sequence and in turn the slowly flowing sequence of images stirs in the reader a sense of organic process, and so one arrives by a logic of images and the rhythm of organic life at the only conceivable end, death. The quiet and powerful inevitability of such poetry is very much like the effect a good film sequence can provide.

Film has, from its earliest days, been aware of and quick to exploit its capacity to present spectacle, and it can do so superbly. Watching *80 Days Around the World* is, in many ways, much more satisfying than world travel. You see all the sights, and from the best vantages, without the dreary hotels, endless railways, bad food, tepid beer, and tired feet. Film spectacles can also be tasteless and boring. Vachel Lindsay saw an early Italian version of *Antony and Cleopatra* which he could only describe as "equivalent to waving the Italian above the Egyptian flag, quite slowly for two hours."[5] A more recent production of the same name is no better but a good deal longer, and both films are dwarfed, in point of spectacle, by Shakespeare's original, with its forty-two scenes, twenty of them in different places, ranging across Italy, Greece, Syria, and Egypt. Great spectacle means more than large sets, splendid costumes, and breathtaking scenery. Great spectacle requires human emotions and actions that are powerful to the point of the spectacular. To give us only the architecture, the scenery, and the costumes, without the great people, is to degrade spectacle into mere sideshow. *Antony and Cleopatra* is a loaded example, of course, but the point holds. Perhaps the finest film spectacle ever done, though not the finest imaginable, is the chariot race in William Wyler's version of *Ben Hur,* which is good because its action, a contest between near-equals, dominates and controls the scenery, the props, and the rhythm of the cutting. The scene is constructed on the pursuit-capture-escape-pursuit formula for excitement that one can find in the novels of James Fenimore Cooper and elsewhere, and which Griffith standardized for the film. Without this controlled human context, all the chariots and horses, the stadium, and all the panoply would have gone to waste. Judging by the average movie spectacle, the film still has an enormous amount to learn from literary spectacle, from the great epics of Homer to Milton.

Writers on film have been quick to point out that one of the distinguishing characteristics of film is its total control over point of view, a control that allows the careful film maker to dictate exactly what shall be seen, and how, and when, and in what context. It is this total control that is said to lie at the root of the film's immense effectiveness, whether as drama or as propaganda. As with many of the techniques or capabilities already mentioned, film does indeed have this control, and it is just as important as is claimed, but it is less new than often appears. Everyone has seen a film at one time or another that begins with the spinning globe, then moves forward until all we see is one continent, then bears in again until we see rivers and mountains, then a city, then the city roofs and streets, and at last the particular building in which the story will start. This method of locating one's subject as a small part of something much larger can be found as early as Chaucer, who used almost exactly the same technique to begin his "Prioress's Tale": "Ther was in Asye, in a greet citee,/Amonges Cristene folk, a Jewerye."[6] First the continent, then the city, then its people, and finally, in the center, a ghetto. The mobility of the movie camera is for us much more noticeable, more visually obvious than its literary counterpart, yet they are the same technique.

More important is the mobility which permits us to see, in a film, the same scene from as many points of view as the director's imagination can suggest, and the technique can obviously lend depth and interest to character study. But this technique is not exclusively the film's either. In the two parts of Shakespeare's *Henry IV*, for example, we see Prince Hal as he sees himself, as his father sees him, as Falstaff sees him, as Hotspur and the Lord Chief Justice see him. Hardy's *The Dynasts* uses a variety of points of view, while Lawrence Durrell's *Alexandria Quartet* is an excellent example of what can be done in literature by carefully turning four radically different angles of vision upon the same series of events.

Currently visible in avant-garde films, especially those of the American West Coast, is the film's capacity for presenting a torrent of images at very high speed. From Lumière's locomotive through the early exploitation of chases and the antics of the Keystone Cops, the film has shown a natural affinity for subjects involving speed, since the medium itself can handle images faster than they can in fact be perceived. Again, this is not so much innovation as it is large scale use of existing techniques. The poetry of John Skelton, for example, goes at breakneck speed, as does the prose of Thomas Nashe or some of the verse of Christopher Smart. Edward Taylor's "Oh do thou sill, plate, ridge, rib and rafter me with grace," or Hopkins' "I caught this morning morning's minion, kingdom of daylight's dauphin, dapple-dawn-drawn Falcon," are other examples of literature's ability to throw out images, one after another, at great speed. Skelton's verse provides a particularly film-like example, the following being from "The Tunning of Elinour Rumming":

The hens run in the mash-fat
For they go to roost
Straight over the ale-joust,
And dung, when it comes,
In the ale tuns.
Then Elinour taketh
The mash-bowl, and shaketh
The hens' dung away,
And skommeth it in a tray
Whereas the yeast is,
With her mangy fistis,
And sometime she blens
The dung of her hens
And the ale together.[7]

Skeltonic verse has no set meter, no set stanza pattern, nothing whatever that is regular. Its sole organizational principle is end rhyme. As C. S. Lewis has noted, Skelton will run a rhyme until the resources of the language are exhausted. Although it is rather primitive poetry, it has at times an odd effectiveness, which Lewis explains by pointing out that the helter-skelter verse seems to work when the subject of the poem is chaos or confusion or bustle.[8] There is, I think, an analogy between Skelton's entertaining verbal clatter and some of the simpler forms of slapstick. Both rely on speed much more than on plot, character, or logic; both rely on simple, obvious, and repeated tricks rather than on nuance or shading. Skelton's short abrupt lines are like short active shots in a Mack Sennett movie, and somehow, when simply strung together, both the movie and the verse are entertaining.

Sheer speed, however, whether in literature or in film, has severe limitations. Thomas Nashe's headlong and breathless prose, which is best perhaps when he is dealing with the bustle of city life, conveys vitality and alertness but little more. And in experimental films, in which images race across the screen, are flashcut, superimposed, arranged into collages and all at a pace that tires the eyes, speed seems to be more an attitude than a subject. It is also a little ominous that the highly developed television commercial, which is close kin to the New American Cinema, also relies more and more on speed, noise, and a blizzard of images. And while Skelton, Nashe, experimental films, and commercials all are effective to a degree, it is arguable that in this attempt to match style to subject, form to content, there is a discernible limit to the now standard critical axiom that form and content should be inextricably interwoven. In all the above cases, it appears that, given enough speed, one need have no content at all, and one then ends up with sheer activity; we are kept so busy merely following that we need have in fact nothing to follow. But speed is only one, and perhaps the extreme, example of a wider aspect of both literature and film, the problem of pace. The film has been gradually re-educating us in matters of pace; the average shot in the average film is now much shorter than it once was. The effect on literature has already been considerable, and in a general way, the question of pace, equally important to both arts, is an area in which each can still learn a good deal from the other.

One of the film's greatest and most often noted assets is its sensitivity to appearance, its built-in capacity to characterize things and people directly, in pictures, rather than through description or analysis. But this advantage cuts two ways, and it is still an open question whether or not the film's total visibility, leaving apparently nothing to the viewer's imagination, will end by paralyzing the imagination. Indeed, most serious film makers seem to recognize the necessity of engaging the spectator's imagination, a typical way to do this being to make succeeding shots not quite consecutive, so that the spectator must fill in the gaps himself. A comic version of this occurs when Charlie Chaplin runs into a pawn shop and reappears immediately with a whole new set of clothes on. It is also true that the bad Hollywood movie that shows us everything and leaves nothing to the imagination (*Gone With the Wind* is an example) tends to be drastically dull. The capacity of the film to characterize directly in pictures is apparently not enough all by itself to make a film interesting.

In this connection it is worth noting that even the technique of characterizing by pictures or images is not new with the movies. A fascinating and sustained attempt to do just that can be found in Nathaniel Hawthorne's *The Marble Faun.* Hawthorne's imagination was always responsive to painting, sculpture, and architecture, as the steady use of and reference to these arts in his work shows, but in the last of his finished romances he attempted and partly achieved something quite remarkable. The book is filled with the visual splendors of Italy, particularly of Rome, and has for this reason been criticized as too much a guide book and not enough a work of fiction. Yet the book can be approached as a quite deliberate attempt to fuse fiction and the visual arts.

Early in the novel, the principal characters meet near the great equestrian statue of Marcus Aurelius, and "its air of grand beneficence and unlimited authority" impresses and awes them. Yet later, when the estranged lovers Miriam and Donatello meet to be reconciled, it is beneath the gently outstretched hand of a statue of Pope Julius the Third in the marketplace at Perugia. Not the Roman Emperor, but the Christian prelate possesses the ability to heal.[9] Hawthorne's careful use of statues here reminds one of the uses to which statues have been put in the films of Eisenstein and Pudovkin, such as the Eisenstein sequence in which three stone lions in different postures are photographed in rapid succession to suggest that the very stones are rising. More to the present point, however, is the fifth chapter of Hawthorne's romance, which is a subtle and effective presentation of Miriam done almost completely in visual terms.

We are given first a sketch of an old Roman *palazzo*, built, like so much of Rome, from yet older buildings, and standing gaunt and still in the heat of the Roman summer. In the courtyard, an old scarred sarcophagus is now a receptacle for trash. A broom sticks out of one corner of it. As one reads along, one becomes slowly aware that this residence is somehow akin to the young woman who lives on its top floor. Both Miriam and the *palazzo* represent some curious, common, but unfathomable confluence of new and old, exotic and common. All this Hawthorne conveys by simply showing us the palace and leading us up its steps with Donatello, who is on his way to visit Miriam. Donatello knocks and is admitted. He and Miriam exchange greetings, but what first catches Donatello's attention is not Miriam. "In the obscurest part of the room Donatello was half startled at perceiving duskily a woman with long dark hair, who threw up her arms with a wild gesture of tragic despair, and appeared to beckon him into the darkness along with her." Donatello, and the reader with him, quickly realize that this is only a wooden model, a "lay figure" used by many nineteenth century artists, but in ways that gradually become apparent, Miriam's model has shown Donatello something about Miriam.

Miriam now gives Donatello a group of her sketches to look over while she finishes a letter. The sketches are of Jael and Sisera, Judith and Holofernes, the daughter of Herodias and John the Baptist, and so on; they are dark, murderous sketches all showing "the idea of woman, acting the part of a revengeful mischief towards man." All the sketches, though, are obscurely flawed. "Her first conception of the stern Jewess had evidently been that of perfect womanhood, a lovely form, and a high, heroic face of lofty beauty; but dissatisfied either with her own work or the terrible story [Jael and Sisera] itself, Miriam had added a certain wayward quirk of her pencil which at once converted the heroine into a vulgar murderess." Donatello turns from these sketches in distress, and now Miriam offers him another pile, this time sketches of "domestic and common scenes, so finely and subtilely idealized that they seemed such as we may see at any moment," but in all these gentle little scenes of courtship and hearth, there is a figure "portrayed apart; now it peeped between the branches of a shrubbery . . . now it was looking through a frosted window, from the outside." The reader need not be told of course that her work. But Hawthorne has one more turn to his idea; as Donatello he is observing, with Donatello, much of Miriam's character from puts aside these sketches also, Miriam goes to her easel and uncovers the picture on it.

> . . . there appeared the portrait of a beautiful woman, such as one sees only two or three, if even so many times, in all a lifetime; so beautiful, that she seemed to get into your consciousness and memory, and could never afterwards be shut out, but haunted your dreams, for pleasure or for pain; holding your inner realm as a conquered territory, though without deigning to make herself at home there.
>
> She was very youthful, and had what was usually thought to be a Jewish aspect; a complexion in which there was no roseate bloom, yet neither was it pale; dark eyes, into which you might look as deeply as your glance would go, and still be conscious of a depth that you had not sounded, though it lay open to the day. She had black, abundant hair, with none of the vulgar glossiness of other women's sable locks; if she were really of Jewish blood, then this was Jewish hair, and a dark glory such as crowns no Christian maiden's head. Gazing at this portrait, you saw what Rachel might have been, when Jacob deemed her worth the wooing seven years, and seven more; or perchance she might ripen to what Judith was, when she vanquished Holofernes with her beauty, and slew him for too much adoring it.[10]

The portrait is, of course, Miriam's self-portrait. What Hawthorne has managed is the presentation of an artist through her own work. And from the wooden dummy through the sketches to the remarkable self-portrait, we are led closer and closer to Miriam, only to be left with a dazzling visual image.

One is tempted to say that this most visual of Hawthorne's works ought to be made into a movie, but it is not clear that the film could achieve the same effect as Hawthorne's prose. For Hawthorne can not only reveal things visually, he can suppress them as well. Thus, much of the effect of this passage lies in our not knowing how stunningly beautiful Miriam actually is until we see the portrait. *The Marble Faun* offers endless material for a discussion of visual effects in literature; the point here is simply that literature had already achieved some unusual and purely visual effects before film even arrived, and while the film's visual characterization is more obvious and indeed much easier to handle, that alone ought to give the film maker pause, lest he content himself with an art of the obvious. The only film I have seen which makes any attempt to control for significance the beauty of a woman (to use an example consistent with Hawthorne's chapter on Miriam) is Agnes Varda's *Cleo from 5 to 7*. Cleo is wigged, dressed, and lacquered like a mannequin or a tart at the start of the film, and when, half way through, she lets down her hair and begins to come alive, her transformation into a lovely and warm woman is carefully and effectively handled. But such effects are rarer than they need be. And a book such as *The Marble Faun*, untypical of nineteenth century fiction though it may be, is full of ideas and experiments to which the film's greater visual capacity has scarcely begun to aspire.

We have dealt so far with visual techniques only, but of course the film must now consider its own way of handling sound. And here too, the very obviousness of the sound, its simple presence in the auditorium, tends to make us forget that literature has long been involved with sound. Early literature was aural, and from Pindar to Ferlinghetti there has always been poetry written to be read or sung. Recently, however, literature, with the exception of the theatre, has become somewhat more silent than it once was. Poetry reading, recitals, even the reading aloud of novels, are less common now than they were a hundred years ago, and indeed, most of modern literature is written to be read silently. The radio play, a completely aural form, represented, until it was killed by television, an interesting and highly promising revival of aural literature, but there is no very generally available aural literature at the moment, unless one considers film and television in this light.

But even aside from oral presentation, one can find in the literatures of all times and countries sophisticated and effective attempts to manipulate sound as part of the literary experience. The commonest way to do this is, of course, the matching of an actual sound with the word describing that sound; thus words like buzz, chirp, and hiss, even when read silently, seem to affect the auditory imagination. The same principle has subtler forms as in Anne Bradstreet's description of "the black clad cricket" or Whitman's "wild ascending lisp" of a carpenter's plane. A splendid use of sound for major dramatic effect occurs in the fourteenth century *Gawain and the Green Knight,* at the point where Gawain is proceeding warily toward his inevitable tryst with the gigantic Green Knight. Gawain walks along gingerly, looking about apprehensively at every turn, and we expect, with Gawain, that we will at any moment see the Green Knight. With our visual expectations steadily growing, it is then marvelously effective when we suddenly hear the harsh grinding of an axe being sharpened on a stone. And this gruesome noise is our introduction to the Green Knight.

In *Huckleberry Finn,* Mark Twain also made careful and extensive use of sound. As many critics have pointed out, the accurate and colorful dialect of the book gives it a special quality, a sense of the actual sound of speech, and many passages, especially those set on the river, show Twain's fascination with sound and his determination to make the book ring with things actually heard. There is the scene in which Huck lies hidden on the island while the steamboat fires its cannon over the water to raise his supposedly dead body; there is the noisy description of a summer storm over Jackson's Island; and there are numerous descriptions of noises heard across the water. "Next you'd see a raft sliding by, away off yonder, and maybe a galoot on it chopping, because they're most always doing it on a raft; you'd see the ax flash, and come down—you don't hear nothing; you see that ax go up again, and by the time it's above the man's head then you hear the k'chunk!—it had took all that time to come over the water."[11]

And James Agee, one of the few men to have done brilliant work in both literature and film, has infused a great deal of his writing with described sounds which give his prose a vivid sense of heard reality. For example, in *A Death in the Family,* the boy Rufus listens to the summer evening as he lies in bed: "All the air vibrated like a fading bell with the latest exhausted screaming of locusts. Couplings clashed and conjoined; a switch engine breathed heavily. An auto engine bore beyond the edge of audibility the furious expletives of its incompetence. Hooves broached, along the hollow street, the lackadaisical rhythms of the weariest of clog dancers, and endless in circles, narrow iron tires grinced continuously after. Along the sidewalks, with incisive heels and leathery shuffle, young men and women advanced, retreated."[12] Here, except for the "grinced" and the "leathery shuffle," Agee seems to be pushing too hard; the passage is a sort of half successful *tour-de-force*. But elsewhere, his control of sound is less obtrusive, stops short of calling attention to itself, and succeeds therefore with remarkable effectiveness:

> It is not of the games children play in the evening that I want to speak now, it is of a contemporaneous atmosphere that has little to do with them: that of the fathers of families, each in his space of lawn, his shirt fishlike pale in the unnatural light and his face nearly anonymous, hosing their lawns. The hoses were attached at spiggots that stood out of the brick foundations of the houses. The nozzles were variously set but usually so there was a long sweet stream of spray, the nozzle wet in the hand, the water trickling the right forearm and the peeled-back cuff, and the water whishing out a long loose and low-curved cone, and so gentle a sound. First an insane noise of violence in the nozzle, then the still irregular sound of adjustment, then the smoothing into steadiness and a pitch as accurately tuned to the size and style of stream as any violin. So many qualities of sound out of one hose: so many choral differences out of those several hoses that were in earshot. Out of any one hose, the almost dead silence of the release, and the short still arch of the separate big drops, silent as a held breath, and the only noise that flattering noise on leaves and the slapped grass at the fall of each big drop. That, and the intense hiss with the intense stream; that and that same intensity not growing less but growing more quiet and delicate with the turn of the nozzle, up to that extreme tender whisper when the water was just a wide bell of film.[13]

Agee's meticulous attention to detail, the gentleness with which he invests the commonplace with grace and beauty, even the careful opening which gives us the speaker's own voice rather than the thoughts of an observer, all combine to give the reader the sensation that he is now hearing for the first time something he has heard all his life without knowing it. It is difficult to think of a film that has taken this much care with sound. Eisenstein used music with fine effect in *Alexander Nevsky,* Hitchcock uses sound well for building up suspense, *Sundays and Cybele* makes free-wheeling and imaginative use of sound, but it remains true that film has rarely gone beyond the device, effective but obvious, of showing the face of the listener rather than that of the speaker. There is a fine example of this in Truffaut's *The 400 Blows,* in which the boy is being harangued by a reformatory official. The boy himself says nothing, but all we see is the boy, restive and uneasy under the barrage of audible stupidity. It is a longish scene, Truffaut's sympathy with the simple and the common is as great and as warm as Agee's, but Agee's craftsmanship is far subtler here than Truffaut's.

Indeed this scene from Truffaut, or the scene in the same director's *Shoot the Piano Player* where the cafe owner rushes to the microphone and sings a silly bouncy little song to cover the noise of a back-room scuffle, are clever uses of sound, pretty much on a par with Robert Browning's gift for presenting us with a long monologue and allowing an ironic picture to form through the speaker's words and despite his intention.

> *Vanity, saith the preacher, vanity!*
> *Draw round my bed: is Anselm keeping back?*
> *Nephews—sons mine . . . ah God, I know not! Well—*
> *She, men would have to be your mother once,*
> *Old Gandolf envied me, so fair she was!*
> *What's done is done, and she is dead beside,*
> *Dead long ago, and I am Bishop since,*
> *And as she died so must we die ourselves,*
> *And thence ye may perceive the world's a dream.*[14]

But for the brilliant and powerful counterpointing that is possible between sight and sound, for an image of two people who speak to each other while they talk to themselves, one must turn to such things as the scene between Lear and the Fool in Act I of *King Lear:*

Fool. . . . Thou canst tell why one's nose stands i' th' middle on's face?
Lear. No.
Fool. Why, to keep one's eyes of either side's nose, that what a man cannot smell out he may spy into.
Lear. I did her wrong.
Fool. Canst tell how an oyster makes his shell?
Lear. No.
Fool. Nor I neither; but I can tell why a snail has a house.
Lear. Why?
Fool. Why, to put's head in; not to give it away to his daughters, and leave his horns without a case.
Lear. I will forget my nature. So kind a father!—Be my horses ready?[15]

Examples could be multiplied indefinitely, but perhaps the above will suffice to make the point that many of the techniques which the film is accustomed to regarding as exclusively filmic are in fact not new, nor are they confined to film. It will be objected that the above comparisons are fanciful, the analogies not really applicable since literature—as printed and as usually experienced—has no pictures and makes no noise. But this is only true in one, and that a superficial, way. For the experiencing of, say, a novel is in large part the experiencing of imagined images and sounds. The film presents actual images and sounds to the spectator, but as noted above, unless these actual pictures and sounds appeal past the eye to the inner eye of imagination they tend to become dull and uninteresting. The literary artist must work harder to stir the imagination, to create pictures and sounds that the reader will actually experience, but the very fact that he must work to achieve such an effect gives him a self-consciousness about what he is doing that many film makers never reach, simply because it is so easy to provide actual images and sounds. When language was new, and words were interesting in and of themselves, one imagines that storytellers or poets needed relatively little artistry to be appreciated. So with the early film. But as we become accustomed even to the exotic (the helicopter in *La Dolce Vita* was a new image, now it has become *de rigeur* in a serious film, and often provokes a laugh from a college audience) the film maker will have to pay as much attention to technique as the novelist or poet.

5 /

Verbal and Visual Languages

FILM, AS WE ARE CONSIDERING IT, IS A NARRATIVE medium and, like literature, is an art based on language. One is accustomed to hearing the word language used rather freely for arts such as painting and architecture, meaning vaguely that the art so described communicates something in some way. But the elements of film narrative, as they have existed since the mid-twenties, form not a figurative but an actual language. Language consists of vocabulary, grammar, and syntax. Vocabulary consists of words, which represent things or abstractions, while grammar and syntax are the means by which the words are arranged. The vocabulary of film is the simple photographed image; the grammar and syntax of film are the editing, cutting, or montage processes by which the shots are arranged. Single shots have meaning much as single words do, but a series of carefully arranged shots conveys meaning much as a composed phrase does. Shots of a house burning, a woman weeping, a plane flying close overhead have each a simple content, but if arranged in the order airplane/house/woman the three together make a statement. Film has an immense, a virtually unlimited vocabulary; its problem has been to evolve a film grammar as subtle as that possessed by even the simplest verbal language. Hence a fade-out followed by a fade-in was early conventionalized to mean "time passes," while a dissolve meant "meanwhile in another place." Irising in and close-ups were originally used as italics or underlining. The silent film, as Balázs observed, has no past tense and no future tense, for pictures alone can express only the present. Flashbacks thus became the standard way to express time past, while future time could be conveyed by misty or slow motion, or "dream" editing. But one of the great benefits of the sound movie was that to the large and expressive vocabulary of the film were added the grammatical and syntactical resources of verbal language. The drawback, unfortunately, was that the film ceased to work to provide its own visual grammar, relying instead on its enormous and subtle vocabulary. What can be achieved by paying close attention to the pictorial composition of each shot with only rather simple editing can be seen in Carol Reed's *Odd Man Out,* John Ford's late and visually idyllic westerns, or Charles Laughton's version of Agee's *The Night of the Hunter.* On the other hand, a film such as *Last Year at Marienbad* could be said to use a limited vocabulary, and an abstact one at that, but a complex grammar of editing techniques so subtle as to evade comprehension more or less successfully.

At any rate, since the introduction of sound, the nature of film language has become more complex. Before sound, as the steady development of film from 1910 to 1925 showed, the visual shot was the basic unit. The single shot was analogous to the word, as Pudovkin saw, while the process of editing supplied the film's grammar. When sound was added to the films, however, the vocabulary of the film was in effect doubled, since it came to consist of both individual sights and individual sounds. As sound enlarged and changed film's basic vocabulary, so it enlarged and gave more variety to film's grammar.

This can be seen most vividly in the matter of verbs. One of the distinguishing marks of effective prose is a high percentage of verbs. Amateur writers, thinking to gain richness and amplitude, fill their prose with adjectives, but prose which lacks strong and frequent verbs lacks energy and movement and is hard to read. One of the reasons why the prose of Samuel Johnson is as effective as it is, despite the heavily Latinate language, is that Johnson uses more verbs than most writers. Now the film had, from the start, a built-in way to obtain the force and the movement which, in prose, comes from verbs. This was the simple fact that one could take pictures of things that were moving. When one photographed a man reaching for a gun on the wall, lifting it down, tucking it under his arm, opening the breach, inserting a shell, and swinging around to face the door, one had an image which requires six verbs to describe in words. Secondly, the camera itself could move, even if the subject stood still. In moving the camera three hundred and sixty degrees around an empty room, one adds the verbal force of turning, seeing, and following to a scene which in reality would be utterly motionless. Thirdly, when the peculiar power of editing had been discovered, film makers found that they had another verbal force at hand. One could join a series of static shots together in such a way as to produce a powerful tension, a sense of latent energy, an expectation of motion that would be hard to describe in prose (though perfectly possible) since one would need language that was at once static but compressed like a spring. Hitchcock is one master of this sort of editing, but it is a common quality in the film. The scenes in *High Noon* in which we are waiting for the train to arrive are a good example of this sort of editing of static material to produce an essentially verbal force. We see the railroad tracks shimmering in the heat, the waiting men, the town clock, the empty streets, the marshal's face. Nothing actually moves, but the editing unobtrusively drives the town toward violence. The fourth sort of verbal force available to the film is, of course, the actual verb on the sound track, where all the dramatic resources of the spoken word are just as available to the film as they have always been to the drama.

Verbs are only one part of speech, to be sure, but they are crucial and one of the reasons why nearly everyone will concede the potential, if not the actual, power of the film may be its rich and varied range of ways to express action as verbs express it in writing.

In addition to the parallels between language and film in matters of vocabulary and simple grammar, but closely connected with that subject, is the use of imagery. It can be argued that all words, even the most abstract, began as images. Emerson points out that "supercilious," cool and abstract as the word is now, means literally "raised eyebrow," and was once a vivid picture of an attitude. So, too, what I have been calling the vocabulary of film is, in ways that are largely obvious (because the film unlike most languages is still young), essentially a repertoire of images. Because language is by nature an image or symbol making process, literature has always been able to make effective, conscious use of it, and there exist, of course, numerous books on the subject. Film too, insofar as it thinks of its material as representations or images of reality and not as slices of life or actual reality, has an equally wide range of possibilties for conscious use of imagery. Film imagery has been, on the whole, rather simple compared with literary imagery, but there are signs that this is changing. It is hard, for example, to think of any film image with the force of, say, Marlowe's description of Helen—"Was this the face that launch'd a thousand ships,/And burnt the topless towers of Ilium?"[1] But the bolder editing that distinguishes the films of the last ten years is gradually increasing the film's command of imagery. One thinks of the profuse imagery of Fellini's recent films or of the subtle and powerful images of desolation which Antonioni drew out of the rocky island in *L'Avventura,* or the wit with which Truffaut made a stale oath come to comic life in a scene in *Shoot the Piano Player:* the hoodlum bragging about his possessions to the unimpressed youngster finally insists, "May my mother drop dead if I don't," whereupon is flashed on the screen an oval shot, framed in lace, of a little old lady keeling over.

Between the film's use of imagery and its literary uses there are both significant similarities and differences. Imagery is used both for vividness and for significance; and one might say that literature often has the problem of making the significant somehow visible, while film often finds itself trying to make the visible significant. Hence the differing emphases within what may be essentially the same technique.

In *Mother,* Pudovkin used film imagery to deepen the effect of a young man's release from prison:

> The son sits in prison. Suddenly, passed in to him surreptitiously, he receives a note that next day he is to be set free. The problem was the expression, filmically, of his joy. The photographing of a face lighting up with joy would have been flat and void of effect. I show, therefore, the nervous play of his hands and a big close-up of the lower half of his face, the corners of a smile. These shots I cut in with other and varied material—shots of a brook, swollen with the rapid flow of spring, of the play of sunlight broken on the water, birds splashing in the village pond, and finally a laughing child.[2]

As we see the scene then, the prisoner looks forward not just to release, but to a world of spring, sun, and water in which one has the freedom of a bird, and the innocence of a child. Or in another way, this could be described as a negative image of prison, the memory of which is to be cleansed by sun and water. A scene that is parallel in some ways to Pudovkin's occurs in the third act of Shakespeare's *Measure for Measure*. Claudio is in prison; his sister has just come to tell him that the price of his release is to be her chastity, and to ask him to die rather than see her dishonored. Shakespeare has Claudio reply:

> *Ay, but to die, and go we know not where,*
> *To lie in cold obstruction and to rot,*
> *This sensible warm motion to become*
> *A kneaded clod; and the delighted spirit*
> *To bathe in fiery floods, or to reside*
> *In thrilling region of thick-ribbèd ice,*
> *To be imprisoned in the viewless winds*
> *And blown with restless violence round about*
> *The pendent world; or to be worse than worst*
> *Of those that lawless and incertain thought*
> *Imagine howling, 'tis too horrible.*
> *The weariest and most loathèd worldly life*
> *That age, ache, penury, and imprisonment*
> *Can lay on nature is a paradise*
> *To what we fear of death.*[3]

These two passages are similar in that each records a prisoner's reaction to the announcement of his fate; each uses the fact and feeling of prison as a basis or a starting point; and each constructs the response as an imaginative flight, a sequence of images. The most interesting difference, though, is that Pudovkin's imagery is, in words, excessively sentimental; only by using pictures can Pudovkin avoid mawkishness. On the other hand, Shakespeare's description has extraordinary force just as it is, in language, while any attempt to redo the scene in pictures would give a surreal effect. Actual filmed images of "thrilling regions of thick-ribbèd ice" would probably only suggest that Claudio is somehow mad. Each scene works in its own medium; neither would work in the other medium; yet the technique is virtually the same in both.

There has been a great deal of discussion about the relative virtues of black and white versus color photography, and it seems generally agreed that widespread adoption of color film for most subjects tends to weaken rather than strengthen the film, since color tends to emphasize the naturalistic, the "real" quality of the image, while black and white makes a subtle but steady insistence that we are watching not reality, but an image of reality. When the color is controlled and made an important aspect of the film experience (*The Red Balloon, Orange and Blue, An American in Paris, The Red Desert*), then, of course, no one would object. But generally speaking, black and white has produced a surprisingly effective style for the film. Among the reasons for this are those cited by Rudolf Arnheim:

> The reduction of all colors to black and white, which does not leave even their brightness values untouched (the reds, for instance, may come too dark or too light depending on the emulsion), very considerably modifies the picture of the actual world. Yet everyone who goes to see a film accepts the screen world as being true to nature. This is due to the phenomenon of "partial illusion." The spectator experiences no shock at finding a world in which the sky is the same color as a human face; he accepts shades of gray as the red, white and blue of the flag; black lips as red; white hair as blonde. The leaves on a tree are as dark as a woman's mouth. In other words, not only has a multicolored world been transmuted into a black-and-white world, but in the process all color values have changed their relations to one another: similarities present themselves which do not exist in the natural world; things have the same color which in reality stand either in no direct color connection at all with each other or in quite a different one.[4]

The fact that we do accept the peculiar, unreal world of black and white is very nearly analogous to the phenomenon which makes a reader accept the world, however strange, of a storyteller, a phenomenon Coleridge called the "willing suspension of disbelief." Further, the black and white world of film is simply a convention, albeit an effective one, in much the same way that verbal language is itself a widely accepted convention. We accept the word for apple as an actual apple much as we accept white hair for blonde in a film. To use E. H. Gombrich's terminology, each is an acceptable substitute for reality.[5]

To turn from the effect of the convention to artistic problems of controlling a convention, the peculiar and unreal relationships that exist in the black and white film world are much like those in language, but they must be recognized before they can be used. In reality, the leaves on a tree bear no relation to a woman's mouth, in film they can be made to bear such a relation. So in language, to use a crude example, objects do not rhyme with one another, but in language they can be made to. Ogden Nash's observation that ants are famous for being active, which is not surprising since no one with formic acid inside would be apt to be calm, is dull enough until the verbal world takes over.

> *The ant has made himself illustrious*
> *Through constant industry industrious.*
> *So what?*
> *Would you be calm and placid*
> *If you were full of formic acid?*[6]

So a routine novel called *The Night of the Hunter* became a powerful work when the world of the evil preacher was presented in a film style that used an almost savage alternation between brilliant whites and deep blacks. It has become common to refer the effectiveness of black and white to its relation to Western morality, but as the above may indicate, it may be more useful to consider it as a convention on the analogy of the convention of language.

Another aspect of film that has been virtually neglected and that may be related to analogous literary problems is the film's essential, but almost invisible, regularity. Film rests, we are told, on an illusion. There is no movement on the screen. The projection process is a matter of projecting a still picture on the screen, then blacking out the screen for a brief time while the machine removes the first still and positions the next. The black mask is then removed and we see the next still. The replacement process occurs twenty-four times a second, but we never "see" the blacked-out screen because of the phenomenon of "persistence of vision"; that is, the image remains on the retina of the eye for a fraction of a second longer than it is there on the screen, just long enough to allow the projector to black out the screen, get another picture in position and let the light through again. The entire process is supposed to be imperceptible; the perfect and subconscious illusion of motion is, for the film maker, an article of faith. But one wonders if the spectator is really totally unaware or unresponsive to what is actually going on before his eyes. Lawrence Durrell, in *Justine*, makes an interesting comment on this: "Are people continuously themselves or simply over and over again so fast that they give the illusion of continuous features—the temporal flicker of the old silent film?"[7]

At any rate, the projection process is completely rigid, utterly regular; nor is this the only rigid aspect of the film. One hears a good deal about the immense mobility and freedom of the film, all of which seems true enough. But one experiences a film under fixed and rigid conditions. One cannot, as with a novel, slow down, speed up, or lay it aside; nor can one, as with a poem, consider it, turn it this way and that, or reread it several times running. Given the immense and often mechanical industry that literary criticism has become, it may be argued that the difficulty one has in actually studying film is to be applauded rather than lamented, but it remains true that the freedom of film form applies more to the film maker than to the viewer. Still, from one point of view, the fixed and immutable form of any given film, as it appears to the viewer, reminds one of some of the stricter literary forms. The sonnet, for example, has a fixed number of syllables, lines, and rhymes; in the hands of Milton or Wordsworth it is carefully enjambed, so that the technically rigid form seems to create or allow a single flowing statement, and a full appreciation of the poem depends upon the reader's being aware of the strict form within which the freely moving poem has been created. One wonders, then, if some aspect of film enjoyment does not arise from similar conditions, from our being vaguely aware of the completely mechanical form within which so much freedom can be somehow apprehended.

Another fixed quality the film has, which will come in for increasing attention as time passes, is its total visibility, a result of the film's inability to reject or ignore surfaces. This aspect of film raises the general problem of the function of detail. The completed work of literature is also fixed—this is not true of oral literature of course—no word can be changed, and from this viewpoint any work of art is complete and unalterable for as long as it lasts. Yet the work of literature can leave certain details to the imagination despite the unchangeable verbal content. A few lines from one of Shakespeare's sonnets will illustrate this:

> *Alas, 'tis true I have gone here and there*
> *And made myself a motley to the view,*
> *Gored mine own thoughts, sold cheap what is most dear,*
> *Made old offenses of affections new.*
> *Most true it is that I have looked on truth*
> *Askance and strangely; . . .*[8]

These lines are vivid and fresh; the images are as alive as the subject, yet there is no distracting detail and nothing to make the poem date. For one thing, the poem does not depend on topical material. The dress, manners, habits, the fashions and fads of the day are simply not used in this sort of writing. The reader, unhampered by detail, can concentrate on the human emotions and the thought involved, and the poem will seem as applicable today as it was three hundred and fifty years ago. Apparently then, it is not true to think that great art requires a completely detailed setting, yet this is what any film is virtually forced to have.

If narrative film relies on a basic film language just as a novel or poem relies on a language, comparison between the two usually works to the film's disadvantage, since film language is not yet as supple, as varied, or as precise as written language. But such comparisons as are possible suggest that the film still has an open line for development in this direction. Film has barely reached the point of having, for example, a conditional tense, a way of showing "what if." In *La Guerre est Finie*, Resnais presents Diego's apprehensive speculations about the future in a series of shots of the same action, but with first one person, then another, first one place and then another. What we see are visual scraps of Diego's musings. Claude Lelouch in his color extravaganza, *A Man and a Woman*, has Anouk Aimée, the heroine, ask Jean-Louis Trintignant what he does. He races cars, but he won't tell her; he will only say that his work is "unusual." At once is cut in a black and white sequence, her amused and deliberately silly speculation, of him as a big city slicker collecting money from a string of B-girls like someone out of Damon Runyon. Resnais seems more concerned than any current film maker with deliberately extending the film's grammar and syntax, yet there remain areas, such as that of generalization, that are still extraordinarily difficult. How, for example, would one get a film equivalent of the famous opening sentence of *Anna Karenina*, "All happy families resemble one another, but each unhappy family is unhappy in its own way." The opening of Jane Austen's *Pride and Prejudice* would present the same problem; "It is a truth universally acknowledged, that a single man in possession of a good fortune must be in want of a wife." Film simply lacks the resources to make such brief generalized speculations. Yet it is perfectly capable of the sort of thing one finds in highly detailed prose. Salinger's description of Seymour's wife as "a girl who for a ringing phone dropped exactly nothing," because it is a description of a particular sight and a particular sound, is a kind of language the film can easily match.[9]

Despite occasional flurries of enthusiasm for what is called abstract film, film in general is not very well suited to abstractions. Samuel Johnson's "Nothing can please many and please long but just representations of general nature" cannot be "said" in film. But if film language has little in common with Johnson's prose, it has somewhat more in common with that of Edward Gibbon; "A candid but rational inquiry into the progress and establishment of Christianity," Gibbon wrote at the start of the fifteenth chapter of *The Decline and Fall of the Roman Empire*, "may be considered as a very essential part of the history of the Roman empire. While that great body was invaded by open violence, or undermined by slow decay, a pure and humble religion gently insinuated itself into the minds of men, grew up in silence and obscurity, derived new vigour from opposition, and finally erected the triumphant banner of the Cross on the ruins of the Capitol." Gibbon's generalization takes a more or less concrete form, the argument proceeds by contrasted images, the elaborate prose is, in fact, a montage composed of several lines of images. This way of writing allows Gibbon to say two things simultaneously. The actual or literal meaning of the above is that while Rome grew weaker, Christianity grew stronger; but the sense that Gibbon's linguistic montage, his ironic juxtaposition of images, gives the sentence is that Christianity attacked and conquered Rome by stealth. A recent CBS documentary called *The Great Love Affair* showed a thorough mastery of this sort of ironic prose montage. Ostensibly about the Americans and their cars, the film was historical and factual. But the montage, the timing, the juxtaposition led one constantly to the film maker's other theme, the auto as the great mechanical curse of modern life. One cannot say then that film is to be compared only with simple prose. It seems more accurate to say that film as yet shows no talent for generalization or abstraction, whereas it is very close to the subtle, controlled, and concrete prose of an ironist such as Gibbon.

Film language seems also to have a hard time with complicated logic; the following bit from Thomas Aquinas is, I would guess, not translatable into film. "To say that a thing is understood more by one [person] than by another may be taken in two senses. First, so that the word *more* be taken as determining the act of understanding as regards the thing understood; and thus, one cannot understand the same thing more than another, because to understand it otherwise than as it is, either better or worse, would be to be deceived rather than to understand, as Augustine argues."[10] Yet this is not to say that the film is incapable of logic. Film logic tends, though, to be either the sort that works by analogy or the sort that draws a conclusion from a mass of evidence. Film has, for example, no trouble with the sort of logic that distinguishes John Donne's famous statement about involvement; "No man is an Iland, intire of it selfe; every man is a peece of the Continent, a part of the maine; if a Clod bee washed away by the Sea, Europe is the lesse, as well as if a Promontorie were, as well as if a Mannor of thy friends or of thine owne were; Any mans death diminishes me, because I am involved in Mankinde; And therefore never send to know for whom the bell tolls; It tolls for thee."[11] This kind of logic of analogy has been used innumerable times in film. A well-known example is the final sequence of *Strike*, which goes, in part:

1. The head of a bull jerks out of the shot, beyond the upper frame-line, avoiding the aimed butcher's knife.
2. The hand holding the knife strikes sharply–beyond the lower frame-line.
3. 1,000 persons roll down a slope–in profile.
4. 50 persons raise themselves from the ground, arms outstretched.
5. Face of a soldier taking aim.
6. A volley of gun-fire.
7. The shuddering body of the bull (head outside the frame) rolls over.[12]

Eisenstein's logic here, like Donne's, is to insist on the truth or applicability of his analogy, the "pacification" of the workers is an act of simple butchery, and the underlying point, much like that of Donne, is that this is wrong because it denies the idea of the human community.

A Japanese film called *The Island* makes a point the reverse of Donne's by the technique of accumulated detail. After an hour and a half of the painful particulars of life on a waterless island, the film's logic, that men are indeed islands, seems inescapable. The logic here is like that of Cassius in *Julius Caesar*, who after a long catalogue of Caesar's physical ailments and shortcomings, has himself and us convinced that he, Cassius, is the better man. As the film has difficulty with abstraction and generalization, so it is weak on abstract or abstruse reasoning, but highly capable of even the subtlest reaches of argument by analogy or illustration.

Since Whitman and the rise of free verse, it has been difficult to draw a clear line between prose and poetry. Indeed, there seems to be no necessary distinction between free verse and prose except that with the former, lines don't always go all the way to the right hand margin. But between classical or regular verse and prose there is a clear distinction which has a bearing on film. Classical or regular poetry, meaning here any kind of verse written in regular, repeated, and predictable patterns of foot, line, and stanza, can have, and, with most good poets, does have two rhythms: the steady metronomic beat of the pattern rhythm, and the spoken, voiced rhythm. Thus the line from Milton's *Samson Agonistes* "Oh dark, dark, dark, amid the blaze of noon," has both a tick-tock iambic pattern and a great sweeping spoken rhythm. The effect, which has been called "the constant evasion and recognition of meter," is really an effect of counterpoint. As in music, one pattern is played against and with another. Thus a double rhythm is possible because of the fixed pattern which a poet adopts to underlie his work. In prose, which has no fixed line length and no necessarily repeated rhythms, this double rhythm cannot be managed, and in this connection film is usually more like prose or free verse than classical poetry. As the sentence is the unit in prose, and the line in free verse, so the shot is the unit in film. And in the absence of a fixed sentence pattern, a fixed line length, or a set shot pattern, all these forms can only achieve a single rhythm. This is not to say, of course, that the single rhythm cannot be superb—one thinks of Donne's sermons, or Whitman's verse, or the well controlled rhythm of Clouzot's *The Wages of Fear*.

Still the film need not be bound to a single rhythm. It would be interesting to see what could be done with a film which decided ahead of time to make all the shots the same length, or which decided to try visual rhyme, that is, making every tenth shot either the same as or very nearly the same as every fifth shot and so on. The effect would probably be very formal, but it would give the film an increased capacity for rhythm; indeed, it would give the film the double rhythm of classical poetry.

In this respect and in innumerable others, only a few of which are touched on above, the film language, which is the basis of film as a narrative art, seems still to be evolving, and it would be premature and rash to suggest that it will not eventually develop a language with the force, clarity, grace, and subtlety of written language. But film language may not evolve so far, or even in this direction; as Resnais has remarked, "the cinema is far from having found its true syntax," and the future of film as language is correspondingly uncertain.[13]

6 /

Film and Modern Fiction

DESPITE THE FACT THAT THE FILM IS STILL evolving and is not in all likelihood a fully realized form, it has already had measurable effects on modern fiction. The most obvious, and in some ways the least significant, of these effects is probably the movie novel, which is now one of the standard sub-genres of fiction and which appears in two main varieties. There is the rags-to-riches tale which undertakes to propel some shapely trull to stardom, and there is the equally vapid though usually well intended sort of novel which chronicles the prostitution of the gifted writer by the nasty old movie industry. Carl Van Vechten's *Spider Boy,* Liam O'Flaherty's *Hollywood Cemetery,* and Christopher Isherwood's *Prater Violet* are all about the ugly, coarse life of the Dream Factory versus the refined sensitivity of the luckless young writer. Recording as they do many a just complaint, it is rather a shame that most such novels have the petulant tone and the silly arrogance that go with most attempts to shoot fish in a barrel. Much more interesting is the sort of thing Charles Van Loan was doing in 1915 and 1916 in the stories which comprise *Buck Parvin and the Movies.* With great gusto and humor, and with a shrewd eye for detail, Van Loan writes stories about the early days of film making. His book is undeservedly neglected, and it catches the spirit of the early and free swinging days of the movies without any of the customary sneering.

More impressive yet are the few attempts to write serious fiction about the films. Pirandello's *Shoot*, subtitled *The Notebooks of Serafino Gubbio, Cinematograph Operator*, Fitzgerald's *The Last Tycoon*, and Nathanael West's *The Day of the Locust* do not comprise the whole list, but are certainly the best of the novels that try to realize the significance of the mechanical and industrial aspects of the movies. Each of these books is ultimately an indictment of the business side of film making, but each also shows, in its technique, the influence of film form. Pirandello's novel moves swiftly, cutting from scene to scene and locale to locale, narrating its story in a manner very much like that of *Birth of a Nation*. Pirandello is especially concerned with the mechanical aspects of filming and he has made his chief character rather eloquent in an attempt to convey in prose the mechanical qualities of film. Gubbio works for the Kosmograph, a monstrous motion picture firm rather like Henry Miller's Cosmodemonic Telegraph Company, and Gubbio, a machine who cranks another machine which devours the reality which is placed before it, is very much aware of the camera's possibilities for dehumanization.

> Already my eyes and my ears too, from force of habit, are beginning to see and hear everything in the guise of this rapid, quivering, ticking mechanical reproduction.
>
> I don't deny it; the outward appearance is light and vivid. We move, we fly. And the breeze stirred by our flight produces an alert, joyous, keen agitation, and sweeps away every thought. On! On, that we may not have time nor power to heed the burden of sorrow, the degradation of shame which remain with us, in our hearts. Outside, there is a continuous glare, and incessant giddiness: everything flickers and disappears.[1]

Pirandello's novel uses film making as a vast metaphor for the modern condition. The tempo, the externality, the machine-like qualities of the world of film are worked into prose and presented in the form of fiction, but it is fiction that is soaked in movie technique.

Fitzgerald was apparently not interested in anything so sweeping. *The Last Tycoon,* in the state in which we have it, is not so much a cinematic novel as it is simply a very good if unfinished novel about Hollywood. Yet from time to time, especially in the flights of language that Fitzgerald occasionally allowed himself, one can see a quality or a technique suggested by the movies. So at the end of the first chapter, after we have met the phenomenal Mr. Stahr, the narrator tries to suggest how he came to be what he is. "He had flown up very high to see, on strong wings, when he was young. And while he was up there he had looked on all the kingdoms, with the kind of eyes that can stare straight into the sun. Beating his wings tenaciously—finally frantically—and keeping on beating them, he had stayed up there longer than most of us, and then, remembering all he had seen from his great height of how things were, he had settled gradually to earth." Stahr is both Icarus and Daedalus, overreacher and inventor; Fitzgerald's image, which takes in Stahr's whole career, is a daring one, and when it continues, we become aware of the deliberate attempt to emulate the camera eye. "I would rather think," the narrator goes on, "that in a 'long shot' he saw the new way of measuring our jerky hopes and graceful rogueries and awkward sorrows, and that he came here from choice to be with us to the end."[2]

Nathanael West's *The Day of the Locust,* a novel overhung with doom and disaster like both the above, is perhaps the most cinematic of the three. The rapid prose, the swiftly alternated scenes, the emphasis on visible detail are here, as in *Miss Lonelyhearts,* most probably evolved from West's own work with films, and in the final scene of the novel West has managed quite an extraordinary effect. His hero has been at work upon a huge painting called "The Burning of Los Angeles." In the last scene, a riot breaks out on the occasion of a premiere and in the delirious mind of the hero the riot merges into the painting. Then, as West describes it, the painting, the riot, the flaming angels of the Apocalypse, and all the prior events and figures of the novel, entered now into the painting as well, rise in one tumultuous moving picture of final destruction.

Everything comes to life, visually and in motion, everything flows into everything else, and the final effect, while it can be tagged surrealist, is actually a triumph of filmic ideas skillfully conveyed in prose.

But one need not confine oneself to Hollywood novels to find writers borrowing movie techniques and upon occasion, improving on them. In *U.S.A.*, for example, John Dos Passos openly tries to expand the resources of the novel by modifying film techniques for the purposes of narrative fiction. The trilogy is fully as ambitious an undertaking as *War and Peace* or *The Dynasts*, and one reason for the enormous range and the rich detail of the work is Dos Passos' use of movie-like collages called "Newsreels" which present all sorts of headlines and news items cleverly juxtaposed to create ironic montages. Newsreel XXII opens:

COMING YEAR PROMISES REBIRTH
OF RAILROADS
DEBS IS GIVEN THIRTY YEARS IN PRISON

There's a long long trail awinding
Into the land of my dreams
Where the nightingales are singing
And the white moon beams . . .

And in sections called "The Camera Eye," Dos Passos shows just how close the literary device known as stream-of-consciousness is to film technique. One such section in *1919* begins:

when the telegram came that she was dying (the streetcar wheels screeched around the bellglass like all the pencils on all the slates in all the schools) walking around Fresh Pond the smell of puddlewater willowbuds in the raw wind shrieking streetcar wheels rattling on loose trucks through the Boston suburbs grief isn't a uniform and go shock the Booch and drink wine for supper at the Lenox before catching the Federal

I'm so tired of violets
Take them all away[3] . . .

A third device in *U.S.A.* is the short biography, the quickly sketched character of a person or an institution. The best known of these is probably Dos Passos' sketch of "The House of Morgan," which in its rapid, detailed, montage-like narrative strongly resembles the technique Orson Welles brought to a similar subject in *Citizen Kane.* André Bazin even ventures that *Citizen Kane* "would never have existed if it had not been for . . . Dos Passos."[4]

More recently, the preface to J. D. Salinger's "Zooey" describes that story, with how much tongue in which cheek would be hard to say, as more of a "prose home movie" than a short story. Salinger's style, at least in "Zooey," is somewhat longwinded, pointedly unedited, documentary in method, and lovingly obsessed with detail. The prose of "Zooey" avoids the technical smoothness one finds in the writing of Updike and Roth as well as in the average Hollywood movie, since Salinger has chosen the seemingly artless and more revealing approach of the amateur who wishes to call attention more to his subject than to his technique. Hence the wondrous avalanche of detail in his description of the medicine cabinet in the story.[5]

Vladimir Nabokov has gone a step beyond this in a story called "The Assistant Producer" which uses the movies as its controlling metaphor and which suggests quite clearly how certain camera tricks and angles can be utilized for prose. The story begins:

> Meaning? Well, because sometimes life is merely that—an Assistant Producer. Tonight we shall go to the movies. Back to the Thirties, and down the Twenties and round the corner to the old Europe Picture Palace. . . . Ghostly multitudes of ghostly Cossacks on ghost-horseback are seen charging through the fading name of the assistant producer. Then dapper General Golubkov is disclosed idly scanning the battlefield through a pair of opera glasses. When movies and we were young we used to be shown what the glasses divulged neatly framed in two connected circles. Not now. What we do see is General Golubkov, all indolence suddenly gone, leaping into the saddle, looming sky-high for an instant on his rearing steed and then rocketing into a crazy attack.[6]

Heinrich Böll's *Tomorrow and Yesterday* makes a similar but subtler use of film, as he shows how the movies have entered so deeply into the imagination of his heroine, Nella, that her imagination henceforward operates in an oddly film-like way. Early in the novel, Nella, in a long series of reflections, calls up and replays for the reader the scraps of her past that have now become like bits of a movie, endlessly replayable reels of frozen memory. Coming home from a stultifying lecture on culture, Nella stops in at the little place where she had first met her husband, Ray, who is later to be killed in the war through the hatred and stupidity of his own commanding officer.

> She had sat there a hundred times with Ray. It was the most appropriate place to patch the film together, and to put the strips—which had now become dreams—into the projector. Lights out, a pressure on the button, and the dream, which had been intended to be a reality, would flash through her head. . . . Now the first sequence could begin. . . . A young man came up to her table, his gray shadow fell on her hand, and before she could look up he said: 'Take off that brown jacket, it doesn't suit you.' Then he stood behind her, calmly lifted her arms and removed her Brown Hitler Youth jacket. He threw it on the ground, kicked it into a corner of the ice cream parlor, and sat down beside her. . . .[7]

Possibly the most impressive of the many attempts to use film material in a novel is James Agee's *A Death in the Family,* which opens with the father, Jay, and his son, Rufus, going off to the movies.

> At supper that night, as many times before, his father said, 'Well, spose we go to the picture show.'
>
> 'Oh Jay!' his mother said. 'That horrid little man!'
>
> 'What's wrong with him?' his father asked, not because he didn't know what she would say, but so she would say it.
>
> 'He's so *nasty*!' she said, as she always did. 'So *vulgar*! With his nasty little cane; hooking up skirts and things, and that nasty little walk!'
>
> His father laughed, as he always did, and Rufus felt that it had become rather an empty joke; but as always the laughter also cheered him; he felt that the laughter enclosed him with his father.

The two attitudes toward Chaplin are a hint of deeper rifts to come between the male and female worlds of the novel. But now we follow Jay and Rufus to the movies: they "found their way to seats by the light of the screen, in the exhilarating smell of stale tobacco, rank sweat, perfume and dirty drawers, while the piano played fast music and galloping horses raised a grandiose flag of dust. And there was William S. Hart with both guns blazing and his long, horse face and his long, hard lip, and the great country rode away behind him as wide as the world." Agee makes the film rise from the screen, he doesn't set the theatre full of people on one side and the film on the other, but makes them almost a single unit, as if William S. Hart were some sort of collective daydream come to life.

But Agee has not brought us to the pictures for the world of wide open spaces, romantic heroes with blazing guns, and ritual plots. What Jay has come to see is now described in the vivid supple prose Agee always brought to his writing on films.

> . . . and then the screen was filled with a city and with the sidewalk of a side street of a city, a long line of palms and there was Charlie; everyone laughed the minute they saw him squattily walking with his toes out and his knees wide apart, as if he were chafed; Rufus' father laughed and Rufus laughed too. This time Charlie stole a whole bag of eggs and when a cop came along he hid them in the seat of his pants. Then he caught sight of a pretty woman and he began to squat and twirl his cane and make silly faces. She tossed her head and walked away with her chin up high and her dark mouth as small as she could make it and he followed her very busily, doing all sorts of things with his cane that made everybody laugh, but she paid no attention. Finally she stopped at a corner to wait for a streetcar, turning her back to him, and pretending he wasn't even there, and after trying to get her attention for a while, and not succeeding, he looked out at the audience, shrugged his shoulders, and acted as if *she* wasn't there. But after tapping his foot for a little, pretending he didn't care, he became interested again, and with a charming smile, tipped his derby; but she only stiffened, and tossed her head again and everybody laughed. Then he walked back and forth behind her, looking at her and squatting a little while he walked very quietly, and everybody laughed again; then he flicked hold of the straight end of his cane and, with the crooked end, hooked up her skirt to the knee, in exactly the way that disgusted Mama, looking very eagerly at her legs, and everybody laughed very loudly; but she pretended she had not noticed. Then he twirled his cane and suddenly squatted, bending the cane and hitching up his pants, and again hooked up her skirt so that you could see the panties she wore, ruffled almost like the edges of curtains, and

> everybody whooped with laughter, and she suddenly turned in rage and gave him a shove in the chest, and he sat down straight-legged, hard enough to hurt, and everybody whooped again; and she walked haughtily away up the street, forgetting about the streetcar, 'mad as a hornet!' as his father exclaimed in delight; and there was Charlie, flat on his bottom on the sidewalk, and the way he looked, kind of sickly and disgusted, you could see that he suddenly remembered those eggs, and suddenly you remembered them too.[8]

The vivid effectiveness of this comes not only from Agee's disciplined and unobtrusive prose, but from the device of describing the movie by describing not only the picture, but also the audience reaction to it. The suggestion is that the film only comes to life or means anything when it has an audience. Opening his novel with this scene, Agee gives the book an unpretentious simplicity. In a way, the whole novel is like a Chaplin film, something that has a broad appeal and an unerring and instinctive hold on human nature. It is fit, too, that Charlie and not William S. Hart stands at the head of the book as an emblem, for *A Death in the Family* is not grandiose, swashbuckling, hero-villain-sweetheart-ridden, but, like the great Chaplin films, is about the little guy, the unheroic man who is always being pushed around by life, but who somehow stumbles along, walking squatly until the "screen shuts over his small image a sudden circle of darkness." Agee is not oblivious to the humor here, far from it, but his concern in this scene and in the book is the same deep note of human sympathy the Chaplin films struck all over the world.

Agee's use of a long movie scene at the start of the novel should alert us to the movie techniques with which the book abounds. I have already referred to the remarkable use of sound Agee managed to make, and in a general way, the book's vividness is largely due to its insistence upon sight and sound. With the Chaplin film still in our minds we read on into the book, seeing and hearing events almost as though we were watching a movie.

A Death in the Family has, spotted throughout, a number of italicized passages which Agee's editors, after his death, positioned in the novel. No one knows where or even if they were going to go in, but they are nevertheless effective since, like the opening passage on the evening hosing of the lawns, they are self-contained episodes, almost sequences, usually of reverie, and since they function chorally or contrapuntally and concern the grand themes of the book, it can be argued that they would work almost anywhere a careful editor put them. They are like dream sequences in a movie or like the final choral sequence of *Eclipse*. It is also arguable that had Agee finished editing the novel himself, these scenes, many of which are frightening and effective in themselves, would have given the novel some of the eerie power of a film called *Rocking Horse Winner*, which was made from a D. H. Lawrence short story about a boy whose mind is destroyed by a brain tumor. At any rate, film themes and film techniques permeate *A Death in the Family* and are partly responsible for the unpretentious power of the book, and for its steady and compassionate commitment to simple humanness.

Malcolm Lowry's *Under the Volcano*, while hardly the same sort of novel as *A Death in the Family*, shows as well a strong film influence, especially in its subtle and varied use of sound. At one point, setting his characters in a bar, Lowry presents the scene as a sound montage. As his characters try to talk, having just met after long absence, bits and pieces of other conversations in the bar float in and register themselves. The effect is weird and uncanny, and Lowry's deft handling of the scene reflects the film writer's constant concern with the uses of sound:

> 'What have you done with your—'
>
> '—life,' came from beyond the glass partition. 'What a life! Christ it's a shame! Where I come from they don't run. We're going through busting this way—'
>
> '—No. I thought of course you'd returned to England, when you didn't answer. What have you done? Oh Geoff—have you resigned from the service?'
>
> '—went down to Fort Sale. Took your shoeshot. And took your Brownings—Jump, jump, jump, jump, jump—see, get it?—'
>
> 'I ran into Louis in Santa Barbara. He said you were still here.'
>
> '—and like hell you can, you can't do it, and that's what you do in Alabama!'
>
> 'Well, actually I've only been away once.' The Consul took a long shuddering drink, then sat down again beside her.

'To Oaxaca.—Remember Oaxaca?'
'—Oaxaca?'
'—Oaxaca.'[9]

Robbe-Grillet, the French novelist, appears to have seized on the film's proclivity for detail and external surfaces, and from this one characteristic (by no means the film's strongest point), to have erected a whole theory of fiction. Distrusting psychology, that is to say, human intentions, motives, and responses, Robbe-Grillet has decided that objects and appearances alone have validity. What we call meaning, he contends, is only due to our artful arrangement of reality into patterns that suit us. In his novels, then, Robbe-Grillet presents only surfaces, only appearances; insofar as he writes about the mind, he only tries to record its fantasies, half-waking states of mind where images drift through, now real, now unreal, now past, now future. Where E. M. Forster wrote "Only connect" in his epigraph to *Howards End,* meaning that the crucial human need is to see how things and people are dependent upon one another, Robbe-Grillet would put "only disconnect." It can be objected that his preoccupation puts him rather in the position of a man who writes books about the folly of writing books, since his dislocations are as carefully worked out as another writer's connections would be, and the result, to judge by his published novels, is a uniform disorder with a high visual content. Thus he makes his point by insisting that he has no point to make, and the result is no better than most attempts to transmute life as it actually is into print, paint, or stone. The opening of *The Voyeur* is a good example of his fiction as drifting cinemism:

It was as if no one had heard.

The whistle blew again—a shrill, prolonged noise followed by three short blasts of ear-splitting violence: a violence without purpose that remained without effect. There was no more reaction—no further exclamation—than there had been at first; not one feature of one face had even trembled.

A motionless and parallel series of strained, almost anxious stares crossed—tried to cross—struggled against the narrowing space that still separated them from their goal. Every head was raised, one next to the

> other, in an identical attitude. A last puff of heavy noiseless steam formed a great plume in the air above them, and vanished as soon as it had appeared.[10]

The sense of discrepancy struck here at the start dominates the novel; it begins and ends in noise that is not heard, violence without purpose or effect, and stares that do not meet. With Robbe-Grillet, it becomes clear that while film may have possibilities for new ways of ordering experience, it also can be, in some hands, a force for disorder, a way of legitimizing randomness, a new and enticing reason to assume that art can and should duplicate the real.

William Burroughs' recent work with verbal collage is still another manifestation of film in literature. Burroughs has tried selecting material, either at random or with some sort of purpose, and then simply juxtaposing the scraps, as a film editor simply joins pieces of film. Substituting juxtaposition for grammar and syntax, Burroughs' work is essentially an exploration of the ways in which montage can be applied to prose. One can read a newspaper column by column, or one can read a given line right across the page. It is not quite clear what significance this latter approach has; it seems to wish to reduce everything to total randomness, an idea which has been brilliantly explored in a story called "The Great Babylonian Lottery" by Jorge Luis Borges. As more and more of life is systematically reduced to dependence on randomness, a remarkable and grim determinism, rather like Calvin's, begins to appear, and when at last everything is left to chance, chance no longer exists. Men are utterly and irredeemably helpless. This does not seem to be Burroughs' intent, however, for his books are warnings, and in the final analysis, seem to be appeals for sanity. The disorders he chronicles in the cinema-derived montage prose of *Naked Lunch* and *Nova Express* are, finally, disorders.

In ways that range from trivial to the very important, then, cinema has already begun to have an effect on fiction. It has provided a few useful techniques for storytelling, such as the flashback, slow motion, the fade, and the dissolve, and it has provided analogies, perhaps even sources for styles, ranging from Salinger's to

Robbe-Grillet's. In a more general way, the film's steady and obvious dependence on point of view seems to have made writers increasingly aware of the uses and possibilities of a controlled and flexible point of view. From Dos Passos, Faulkner, and Hemingway to the present, strict control of point of view has become increasingly important in fiction; this is due at least in part to the example of film. In other ways, film's narrative economy seems to have impressed some novelists, and its total visibility has put an increased emphasis on sight and sound in fiction.

Arnold Hauser has made a more sweeping speculation. "One has the feeling," he writes, "that the time categories of modern art altogether must have arisen from the spirit of conematic form, and one is inclined to consider the film itself as the stylistically most representative though qualitatively perhaps not the most fertile genre of contemporary art."[11] This is a little vague and very probably overstated. Yet as the movies have become a part of modern life, they have indeed been swept into fiction as material or subject matter, as in Walker Percy's *The Moviegoer*. Secondly, the movies' peculiar way of seeing and presenting modern life has also found frequent reflection in fiction. Thus Norman Mailer can use the camera eye for detail in a passage such as this from *The Naked and the Dead*: "Almost all the tents were down in the bivouac area, and here and there a soldier would go skittering through the mud, staggering from the force of the wind with the odd jerking motions of a man walking in a motion picture when the film is unwinding too rapidly."[12] Finally, one must consider the general influence of film narrative on fictional narrative. As early as 1934 Ezra Pound was moved to declare that "the cinema supersedes a great deal of second-rate narrative," and that "a film may make better use [than other forms] of 60 percent of all narrative dramatic material."[13] Extreme at the time they were written, these claims no longer seem outrageous, and while film has come to share with fiction the field of narrative or simple storytelling, film is also exerting a powerful influence on the other and still major narrative form.

7 /

The Question of Order and Coherence in Poetry and Film

THE FILM'S BASIC TECHNIQUE, THE METHOD OF composition by juxtaposition which can be called cutting, editing, or montage and which is the most characteristic feature of film form, is also the aspect of film that has had the greatest impact on literature. The excesses into which this technique can lead are most evident in the work of Robbe-Grillet and the numerous writers who see as he does a mandate for chaos in the film's technique of juxtaposition, while the greatest constructive uses of montage in literature are to be found in modern poetry.

Early in the century, Vachel Lindsay wrote a long poem called "The Trial of the Dead Cleopatra in Her Beautiful and Wonderful Tomb," and in his *Art of the Moving Picture* suggested that the poem be made into a film. It is I think a poor poem, but Lindsay's idea is arresting. Pursuing his claim that the picture language of the silent film is analogous to the hieroglyphics of the Egyptians, Lindsay pushes the comparison even further. Like Melville before him, Lindsay came to believe that man's myths and religions can all be traced to Egypt. Melville noted that the "awful idea of Jehovah" was born in the pyramids, and Lindsay wrote that "Man is an Egyptian first, before he is any other type of civilized being."[1] Thus Lindsay proposed to take the *Book of the Dead,* which he translated as "On Coming Forth by Day," to retell the Cleopatra story through the form and rituals of this book and thus produce a sort of prototype or archetype of resurrection. The Christian and Egyptian myths are crucial, of course, but one also gets the impression that Lindsay thought the film capable of a sort of visible, if mechanical, proof or demonstration of the idea of immortality.

As Shakespeare could urge in his sonnets that the writing of poetry combats time, denies ruin, and confers a renewal of sorts because artistic creation is itself a process of renewal, so Lindsay seems to have felt that the motion picture was itself a pattern or a paradigm of rebirth or renewal. Emerson once wrote that "genius is the activity that repairs the decay of things," and Lindsay's poem, odd and flawed as it appears, still represents a noble example of such activity.

Perhaps the best of the scattering of poems that owe an obvious debt to films in one way or another is Hart Crane's "Chaplinesque." Not only has Crane here, as in so many other places, used the condensed elliptical style which is so similar to the flow of images in a film, but more importantly, it is the visible humanity, the sense of grace, perceived and conveyed in what Lindsay called a "quietness of light," that shows how deeply the films had affected Crane:

The game enforces smirks; but we have seen
The moon in lonely alleys make
A grail of laughter of an empty ash can,
And through all sound of gaiety and quest
Have heard a kitten in the wilderness.

Crane also used the image of the cinema at the very start of his most ambitious poem, *The Bridge.* In the third stanza of the "Proem" occur these lines:

I think of cinemas, panoramic sleights
With multitudes bent toward some flashing scene
Never disclosed, but hastened to again,
Foretold to other eyes on the same screen.[2]

Crane seems to suggest here that the poem itself will be a series of flashing scenes and panoramic sleights, a poem of film-like images easier to witness than to comprehend. Crane's poetry remains difficult, but if it is thought of as using certain elements of cinema style, it becomes a little easier to make out.

Interesting as the above poems—and others like them—may be in their obvious attempts to include film forms and film subjects in poetry, the actual significance of such overt influence is small by comparison with some other and much broader matters of style which have deeply marked both modern poetry and the film without its being at all easy to say which has influenced which. However one manages to explain it, though, it can be argued that modern poetry and the film have been evolving along surprisingly similar lines.

Earlier it was suggested that Whitman's poetry can be considered a step toward cinema style. But it is, of course, true that Whitman's example was not widely followed in the nineteenth century, nor did his increasingly bardic pose, nor his later and inflated verse, encourage imitation, and poetry in America from the Civil War to the turn of the century continued to grope with problems of form in a world that seemed to have less and less form itself. Sidney Lanier tried to push poetry into pure music; Poe had also worked to this end; Emily Dickinson created her magnificent poems in part by resorting to a form that was based on hymnody; Melville tried all sorts of strange verse forms; and Stephen Crane experimented with a harsh gnomic style. Meanwhile the poets who inherited the genteel tradition of Bryant, Longfellow, Whittier, and Lowell stayed within conventional forms and styles while their work grew increasingly weak and unreal. By the 1890's a poet such as Edwin Arlington Robinson could look around him and see nothing but what he called the "little sonnet men," the gentlemen poets with three names and tired themes. Robinson's own work, which continued up into the thirties, but which remained characteristic of his earliest writings, is in some ways very revealing about the general state of poetry from 1890 to 1910. Robinson's ruling image, one which occurs over and over in his poems, is the image of the loss of light. One sees it clearly in "Credo," written in 1896:

I cannot find my way: there is no star
In all the shrouded heavens anywhere . . .
No there is not a glimmer, nor a call,
For one that welcomes, welcomes when he fears
The black and awful chaos of the night.[3]

The idea is worked out in greater detail in "The Man Against the Sky," in which the loss of light is quite clearly an image of the loss of certainty and direction. Robinson himself, as Robert Frost remarked, was a poet who "stayed content with the old way to be new," meaning that Robinson avoided radical formal innovation, preferring to treat new problems with forms that had been in use for hundreds of years. But Robinson's reflective, almost Wordsworthian temperament had difficulty even with the old forms, and his work lacks color, lacks visibility, prefers to present endless dialogue and colloquy rather than scene, or action, or picture, and is heavily verbose and abstract. His poems are poems of discursive rationality, dominated by the logic of prose, though they are set, rather uneasily one feels, in the form of verse. Thus Robinson's theme, the waning of the light, and his practice, the pervasive haunting and intentional flatness of what one constantly feels ought to be better seem to mark, between them, a sort of low point in modern poetry. The problem, I think, was essentially one of form, and Robinson's shrewd insistence on the fading light constitutes a brilliant diagnosis of what was wrong. For if the image for the technical sterility of the turn of the century was darkness, the new poetry of the period roughly from 1912 to 1925 signalized its arrival by a fresh insistence on light. The poetry of Pound, the Imagists and Amygists, Eliot, Williams, Stevens, and others used new forms, sought new voices, and insisted on highly visual imagery; through it all crept the image of light as a counterforce to Robinson's image of darkness.

At the same time the film began to find itself, and it too was working with new forms, and insisting on high visibility. Because its art consists of painting with light, it was also, in its way, flushed with optimism and fascinated with the phenomenon and even the imagery of light. By 1920, the new poetry had more in common with film than it had with Robinson and all that Robinson stood for in poetic expression. The new poetry and the film had both found fresh and exciting ways to approach their material, and both seemed, at the time, to have found a way around the questions of meaning that had so tormented, say, "The Man against the Sky." For neither the film nor the new poetry seemed to care to explain about what things meant. It was enough, as it had often been enough for Whitman, simply to present images, to celebrate life. Wallace Stevens dramatized the problem of conventional meaning and a possible solution or way round the problem in a poem which begins:

Twenty men crossing a bridge,
Into a village,
Are twenty men crossing twenty bridges,
Into twenty villages,
Or one man
Crossing a single bridge into a village

This is old song
That will not declare itself . . .

If one asks what twenty men crossing a bridge mean or what they really are, one can reply by saying that since each man sees the bridge differently, then for each the experience is different and therefore cannot be generalized. Or one can say that all men are essentially alike and therefore any man's experience in crossing a bridge is the same as any other man's. But neither of these psychological explanations really tells us anything worth knowing; they are abstract formulations. The poem continues:

Twenty men crossing a bridge,
Into a village,
Are
Twenty men crossing a bridge
Into a village.

That will not declare itself
Yet is certain as meaning . . .

One could explain by saying that the thing means itself. Twenty men crossing a bridge are no more and no less and no other than twenty men crossing a bridge. That then is clear enough, but it still doesn't justify all the fuss, nor does it get us anywhere. If things are what they are, then there is nothing to do except, with Gertrude Stein, to go round and round. Finally Stevens' poem finds, and illustrates, the way out of the problem:

The boots of the men clump
On the boards of the bridge.
The first white wall of the village
Rises through fruit-trees.
Of what was it I was thinking?
So the meaning escapes.

The first white wall of the village . . .
The fruit-trees . . .[4]

Stevens cuts into the scene below the abstract or generalized statement. A particular sound and a particular sight serve instead to create an image in the mind, a remembered scene composed of remembered details. It is the experience, the actuality of the scene, that matters; and as the scene becomes visible and audible, it becomes enough, it is sufficient in and of itself, and so it is no matter, and perhaps even a good thing, that the meaning escapes. This is not to say, of course, that the poem is without significance or importance, for it has both. The poem's close brings to mind an image like those of the impressionist painters, and the world, when it is seen by such men and passed on for us to see without what Keats called the "irritable reaching after fact and reason" is a marvelous and splendid place, rich and full in itself, making it enough just to be alive and aware.

As it has been explored and presented, this strong and widespread interest in the sights and sounds of the world, and the accompanying decrease of interest in explaining or reasoning it all out, has given modern poetry and film a whole world, one that is quite new in that it is now for the first time widely seen and shared. And both film and poetry have contributed to our understanding of this realm, which is essentially one of sight and sound; in which significance arises from all sorts of things but rarely from plain statement. Significance arises from context, from juxtaposition, from irony, from image, from overtones, or hints. Both film and modern poetry seem to agree that the point is not to tell the spectator or reader what things mean, but to make him find, feel, or realize the meaning for himself. Thus the realm in which film and poetry now move is not a realm of fixed values, not a realm of prose logic or discursive intelligence.

Just how close the techniques of the experimental or innovative line of modern poetry are to those of film, particularly the silent film, may be seen by considering T. S. Eliot's preface to and translation of St. John Perse's *Anabasis*. Eliot describes the poem as a "series of images of migration, of conquest of vast spaces in Asiatic wastes, of destruction and foundation of cities and civilizations. . . ." Eliot speaks of the poem's "logic of imagery" and he explains that "any obscurity of the poem, on first readings, is due to the suppression of 'links in the chain,' of explanatory and connecting matter, and not to incoherence, or to the love of cryptogram. The justification of such abbreviation of method is that the sequence of images coincides and concentrates into one intense impression of barbaric civilization. The reader has to allow the images to fall into his memory successively without questioning the reasonableness of each at the moment; so that, at the end, a total effect is produced." *Anabasis*, as Eliot so clearly points out, is not built upon meter or rhyme or other forms of verbal regularity; its order, like that of a film, is a "logic of imagination," a logic of carefully arranged sequences of images in Whitmanesque lines. The poem, in Eliot's version, begins:

> I have built myself, with honour and dignity have I built myself on three great seasons, and it promises well, the soil whereon I have established my Law.
>
> Beautiful are bright weapons in the morning and behind us the sea is fair. Given over to our horses this seedless earth,
>
> delivers to us this incorruptible sky. The Sun is unmentioned but his power is amongst us,
>
> and the sea at morning like a presumption of the mind.[5]

After the initial sentence, which gives us a speaker, a premise, and a purpose, the lines turn to the business of simply delivering images of arms, of morning, of the sea, of horses, earth, sky, and sun, much as a good film lays out its significant spaces and forces at the start. It is by no means clear that *Anabasis* shows any actual or demonstrable film influence, yet its remarkable closeness to techniques and approaches made familiar in this century by the film makes this poem, and a good deal of modern poetry, close kin to film.

The tendency of both modern poetry and film to display, disclose, or reveal their subjects rather than to explain or judge them can also be seen clearly in the steadily increasing importance of documentary styles in film and in poetry. Russian directors in the twenties often used citizens rather than actors in an effort to avoid the appearance of artifice; war films use newsreel clips for action sequences; *Citizen Kane* exhibits an overtly documentary technique, while Italian Neorealism and the movement known as *Cinéma Vérité* show that this emphasis on authenticity and simplicity through documentation is far from spent. Documentary film undertakes to edit reality. It avoids clever or tricky shots, concentrates on sober camerawork, relying for its effect on the authenticity of its material, and depends more on the perception of the cameraman than on the skill of the editor. Poems such as William Carlos Williams' *Paterson*, Ezra Pound's *Cantos*, MacLeish's *Conquistador*, Berryman's *Homage to Mistress Bradstreet*, and even such poems as Lowell's "The Quaker Graveyard in Nantucket" and Eliot's "The Waste Land" share this technique. All depend heavily on written documents which are inserted into the text, often making up a substantial part of the text. Each of the poems is reaching for greater authenticity by including historical records, diary entries, and fragments of other poems, but of equal importance with the documentary material is the arrangement of such material in the poem. In film, documentary techniques are usually intended to bring out or stress the actual, real, or tangible qualities of the subject. In literature, documentary techniques serve this purpose too, but it is less noticed than its other effect, which is to provide some sort of connection between past and present. But despite the apparent realism of film documentary and the apparent historicism of documentary poetry, the so called documentary approach need be neither realistic nor historical, for in the film, material is rigorously selected to illustrate the film maker's point and in poetry the past is presented and documented with a very careful, not to say loaded, selectivity. In each form, though, an appearance of realism or historicism is given to the modern work of art, whose essential principle may be neither realistic nor historical. Indeed, in documentary as in other respects, both modern poetry and film seem to insist primarily on the integrity of the design of any given work.

William Carlos Williams' "Classic Scene" is an example of one rather obvious concern with design:

A power-house
in the shape of
a red brick chair
90 feet high

on the seat of which
sit the figures
of two metal
stacks—aluminum—. . . [6]

Robert Frost wrote a number of poems that make conscious use of design, one of them a little-known sonnet:

She is as in a field a silken tent
At midday when a sunny summer breeze
Has dried the dew and all its ropes relent,
So that in guys it gently sways at ease,
And its supporting central cedar pole,
That is its pinnacle to heavenward
And signifies the sureness of the soul,
Seems to owe naught to any single cord,
But strictly held by none, is loosely bound
By countless silken ties of love and thought
To everything on earth the compass round,
And only by one's going slightly taut

In the capriciousness of summer air
Is of the slightest bondage made aware.[7]

Yeats' concern for design led eventually to the extravagance of *A Vision,* with its perfect symmetry and its elaborate detail. The book is a vast design, almost a cosmology, that Yeats said served to give him a source for metaphors. And Wallace Stevens has carried on this attention to design in such poems as "The Anecdote of the Jar":

I placed a jar in Tennessee,
And round it was, upon a hill.
It made the slovenly wilderness
Surround that hill. . .[8]

This sense of design, of pattern, which I suppose can be thought of as some sort of organizing principle other than the narrative or linear, has been equally evident in the film. The four stories and the keystone image of *Intolerance* are an attempt, if not a wholly successful one, to make design dominate the material. Eisenstein's *Strike* and his *Potemkin* show a strong sense of design; Eisenstein once noted that the latter film came to him as he was gazing one day at the great Odessa steps, and the film was then built around those steps. The same director's *Ivan the Terrible* has an even greater, almost oppressive, sense of design. *Citizen Kane* also works because of its careful design; if it is a film about men, its design is organized around buildings. The list could be extended indefinitely; the work of Disney, McLaren, Hitchcock, Cocteau, and Resnais is all marked by as strong an insistence on design as that in modern poetry.

Closely allied with this sense of design, and strongly reinforced by a critical movement loosely called the New Criticism, is the idea, most easily observed in poetry and in film, that a work of art is, and should be, largely self-sufficient. The poem, or the film, the argument goes, provides its own context, encloses its own world, is its own frame of reference. Its own arrangement, its tensions and structure, its text alone constitute it whole, and one need not refer beyond the text to history, biography, or the real world. Thus in a famous phrase, Archibald MacLeish has said "A poem should not mean/But be."[9] A simple example is a poem of Richard Wilbur's called "Piazza di Spagna."

> *I can't forget*
> *How she stood at the top of that long marble stair*
> *Amazed, and then with a sleepy pirouette*
> *Went dancing slowly down to the fountain-quieted square;*
>
> *Nothing upon her face*
> *But some impersonal loneliness—not then a girl,*
> *But as it were a reverie of the place,*
> *A called-for falling glide and whirl;*
>
> *As when a leaf, petal, or thin chip*
> *Is drawn to the falls of a pool and, circling a moment above it,*
> *Rides on over the lip—*
> *Perfectly beautiful, perfectly ignorant of it.*[10]

The poem catches a moment. It does not matter who the girl is, what her relation to the speaker is, when or where it happens, what preceded, or what is to follow this one moment. The title is a sort of connection between the poem and the world, but it is not much of one. Any flight of steps would do as well. The girl gains nothing from Rome. The delight of such a poem is in the way the lines themselves create and contain the momentary preoccupation perfectly. The verse is light, as is the girl's movement. The poem is not sonorous or ponderous because to be so would contradict the tone of the moment. The poem's economy is perfect, and it itself is as graceful and pleasing as the moment described. One could go on, working with more complicated matters of diction, rhythm, and so forth, but the point is clear enough. The poem is designed to be self-sufficient and it is. The film has not gone as far as poetry has toward the ideal of the self-contained work, but such films as the various parts of *Fantasia*, Bergman's *The Magician*, Resnais's *Last Year at Marienbad*, and Cocteau's *Blood of a Poet* are in this same tradition.

To be thus self-sufficient, a given work must have a strong design to hold it together. The result, whether in film or poetry, is a tendency to regard a given movie or a given poem more as an artifact, as a verbal or pictorial construct, than as a work meant primarily to communicate something to someone. As Frank Kermode has pointed out, with the elegant simplicity and common sense that mark his work, "Information cannot be conveyed where there is no scope for choice between understood alternatives."[11] So when Michael Drayton begins a sonnet with—

Since ther's no helpe, Come, let us kisse and part,
Nay, I have done: You get no more of Me,
And I am glad, yea glad with all my heart,
That thus so cleanly, I my Self can free...[12]

—the reader knows at once what is going on, since he is aware not only of what Drayton says, but of what he does not say, of what is sayable about the situation. Everything is clear because we understand the alternatives. But can a reader grasp, in a similar way, a poem which goes:

so much depends
upon
a red wheel
barrow

glazed with rain
water

beside the white
chickens.[13]

The poem has a point, of course, for much does depend on our ability and our willingness to see the world around us, to be aware of color, of contrast, of unpretentious things, to appreciate the difference between design and accident. But none of this is quickly or even surely communicated, no alternatives are visible or even imaginable. We do not know where to start. If so much depends on this, what might be an example of something on which nothing depends?

No doubt the weakening of poetry as a communicative art (and as a narrative art) is offset to some extent by the heightened beauty and interest of the poem as artifact, but it remains true that such an ideal of self-sufficiency depends heavily upon the order and design that can be achieved in the individual work, and it is ironical that one of the great themes of modern poetry and film as well has been the theme of the breakdown of order and design.

8 /

Waste Lands: The Breakdown of Order

THE IDEA OF THE LOSS OF ORDER HAS BECOME SO familiar a theme that if it is not precisely a part of the modern scheme of things, it is at least a stable, well recognized, and quite conventional assumption. The loss of inherited values, the chaotic fluidity of the social order, the weakening of once firm theologies, sciences, and intellectual methodologies, the disappearance of goals, and the dubiousness about identity are both symptoms and causes of a widespread sense of disorder. And in modern poetry, the very poets to whom design has meant so much are the ones who have perceived most clearly the disappearance of any order higher than that of mere design. One well-known statement is Yeats' "The Second Coming":

Turning and turning in the widening gyre
The falcon cannot hear the falconer;
Things fall apart; the centre cannot hold;
Mere anarchy is loosed upon the world,
The blood-dimmed tide is loosed, and everywhere
The ceremony of innocence is drowned;
The best lack all conviction, while the worst
Are full of passionate intensity.[1]

"The Second Coming" is a carefully designed poem about the failure of common and visible order. Yet the poem ends by asking "And what rough beast, its hour come round at last,/Slouches toward Bethlehem to be born?" Simple orderliness is apparently dispelled and displaced by a greater but infinitely more deadly sort of order, akin perhaps to the Greek idea of Necessity. Robert Frost has also written a chilling poem in which, with his customary irony, he wonders at last if such order as may exist is not indeed quite lethal:

I found a dimpled spider, fat and white,
On a white heal-all, holding up a moth
Like a white piece of rigid satin cloth—
Assorted characters of death and blight
Mixed ready to begin the morning right,
Like the ingredients of a witches' broth—
A snow-drop spider, a flower like a froth,
And dead wings carried like a paper kite.

What had that flower to do with being white,
The wayside blue and innocent heal-all?
What brought the kindred spider to that height,
Then steered the white moth thither in the night?
What but design of darkness to appall?—
If design govern in a thing so small.[2]

A poem, as Frost once said, is "a momentary stay against confusion." Thus perhaps the most ominous of the modern poetic statements or documents of chaos is T. S. Eliot's warning in "East Coker" that language itself seems to be decaying:

. . . And so each venture
Is a new beginning, a raid on the inarticulate
With shabby equipment always deteriorating
In the general mess of imprecision of feeling,
Undisciplined squads of emotion.[3]

In the film one can also find a steady concern with this loss of order. From *The Cabinet of Dr. Caligari*, and *Un Chien Andalou*, and *L'Age d'Or* to *La Dolce Vita, L'Avventura, Mondo Cane,* and *Dr. Strangelove,* the film has borne consistent witness to a world in which entropy rules, order dissolves, and the grotesque becomes the normal. It can be argued that this relaxation of order has reached even further, undermining the design and pattern of the work of art itself. Ezra Pound's great work, *The Cantos,* has apparently foundered because of the absence of a sufficiently large organizing principle. The same can be said for William Carlos Williams' *Paterson,* a long poem which went on and on, like life itself, unable to find or to fulfill its pattern. So Hart Crane's *The Bridge,* a deliberate attempt to bridge gaps and perceive order, failed even to order itself as a poem. Yeats' late poem "The Circus Animals' Desertion" chronicles the successive failures of Yeats' various masks and designs, and one might even claim that Eliot's "The Waste Land" and Robert Lowell's "The Quaker Graveyard in Nantucket" are triumphs of the attempt to write significant poetry without resorting to any sort of clear order, pattern, or design. So in the film, from *Intolerance* and *Greed* to *Ivan the Terrible, 8½, Eclipse,* and *The 400 Blows,* one can find innumerable films which are undeniably fine works and which seem deliberately to have avoided or submerged any visible or obvious order or pattern.

This sense of a lost order has been so strong and has had such a pervasive effect on the arts that one of the commonest images for our times is the image of the wasteland. From the ash heaps in *The Great Gatsby* to the desolations of Ravenna in *The Red Desert,* modern narrative art has maintained that this is a dry time, a barren and sterile place, and that we lead empty and futile lives. And two of the artists who have dealt most honestly and most thoroughly with this theme or image are T. S. Eliot and Federico Fellini. Though working at different times, in different countries, and in different mediums, they have still a surprising number of things in common. Indeed some of their work is so similar in theme, approach, and even technique that the work of each can to some extent illuminate that of the other. To put it simply, Fellini's films depend heavily on what are usually thought to be solely poetic techniques, while Eliot's poetry makes frequent use of certain cinematic techniques. We have already seen Eliot describing Perse's *Anabasis* as a verbal montage. It takes little insight to see that this also applies to Eliot's own poems, especially to "The Waste Land." Fellini, on the other hand, has been quoted as saying, "Movies now [1965] have gone past the phase of prose narrative and are coming nearer and nearer to poetry. I am trying to free my work from certain constrictions—a story with a beginning, a development, an ending. It should be more like a poem with metre and cadence."[4] Eliot's poetic practice thus leans toward cinema style, Fellini's toward poetic style, and it is not, therefore, surprising that there are numerous suggestive parallels to be found in their work.

Both "The Waste Land" and *La Dolce Vita,* for example, have been unusually successful in that each has seized the imagination of a large audience, and each has become almost an epitome of the outlook of a generation. Critics continue to complain that they are poorly structured, chaotic, difficult, and even private or idiosyncratic, but despite these objections, there is a quality in each work which has made it popular or available. Each has been widely quoted and imitated; the title of each has entered common speech. And if one thinks of "The Waste Land" as a poem written as a film-like sequence of images and of *La Dolce Vita* as a filmic poem, a film designed with the complexity, structure, and texture of a modern poem, each work will seem less difficult or capricious. Each is episodic, "The Waste Land" being made up of five detached and individually titled sections, "The Burial of the Dead," "A Game of Chess," "The Fire Sermon," "Death by Water," and "What the Thunder Said." *La Dolce Vita* is also composed of semidetached sequences, long scenes which are not always clearly related to one another. There is the encounter with Maddalena, the Field of the Miracle, the Steiner episode, the sequence centered on Sylvia, the scene with Marcello's father and Fanny, and the two contrasted and final parties, one at the home of the desiccated aristocrats, the other at a modern seaside villa. There is little strict narrative continuity in either work. Indeed neither is really narrative in any important sense. Each is a continuous succession of scenes and images which build up impressions only cumulatively, impressions which are neither complete nor fully comprehensible until the end.

Both the film and the poem are twentieth century versions of Ecclesiastes, visions of the hollowness of contemporary life. The hero or central figure of each is a suitably ambiguous figure. Tiresias, in "The Waste Land," is called by Eliot, in a note appended to the poem, a "mere spectator and not indeed a 'character,' . . . yet the most important personage in the poem, uniting all the rest. . . . What Tiresias *sees,* in fact, is the substance of the poem."[5] In *La Dolce Vita,* the central character fulfills much of the same role. What Marcello, the reporter, sees, is the substance of the film. He, too, is more a spectator than a character, though he is also the latter, and he, too, is the personage who unites the other characters. Everything that the others act out is somehow a part of Marcello's personal world. (The figure of Tiresias in "The Waste Land" is also paralleled, in other repects, by the strange prophet named Bhisma, who is half-man and half-woman, and who plays an important part in Fellini's later *Juliet of the Spirits*). Tiresias in "The Waste Land" and Marcello in *La Dolce Vita* stand at the center of and preside over a series of incidents, encounters, and memories, having largely to do with religion and sex. Eliot's poem ranges from the affair between Elizabeth and Leicester to a scene which relies on Shakespeare's *Antony and Cleopatra* and Pope's *The Rape of the Lock,* to a tawdry assignation in a flat, to the sex-centered pub scene between Albert's wife and her "friend," to the hyacinth girl and her earlier innocence and youth, all united in and seen by the androgynous figure of Tiresias. So Marcello, in the film, witnesses or takes part in a variety of sexual encounters or attempts. There is the scene with Maddalena in the prostitute's flat; several scenes between Marcello and his cloying maternal mistress, Emma; his infatuation with Sylvia the American movie star; the pathetic encounter between Marcello's father and Fanny; and Marcello's increasingly desperate sexual forays in the closing scenes. The cumulative effect of all this is as wearisome and as meaningless for Marcello as it was for Tiresias, whose description of himself is also a decent description of Marcello:

> *His vanity requires no response,*
> *And makes a welcome of indifference.*
> *(And I Tiresias have foresuffered all*
> *Enacted on this same divan or bed;*
> *I who have sat by Thebes below the wall*
> *And walked among the lowest of the dead.)*
> *Bestows one final patronising kiss,*
> *And gropes his way, finding the stairs unlit. . . .*[6]

As each work accumulates a range of sexual encounters but finds it all less than satisfying or fulfilling, so each explores a like variety of religious scenes and concerns. Eliot takes a different tone on this subject from Fellini, and does not insist, as does Fellini, on the total poverty and emptiness of religion. From the Ascension by helicopter at the start of the film to the scene in which Anita Ekberg, dressed in parody of a priest, skylarks to the top of St. Peter's, from the long sequence on the Field of the Miracle to the sequence in which Steiner's great religious organ music serves as a prelude to his ugly suicide and the killing of his children, Fellini is, in what is probably the heaviest handed and least balanced aspect of the film, attacking the worn out religiosity of Rome. One possible exception to this might be the breaking up by thunderstorm of the elaborate, phony, and infinitely seamy and corrupt exploitation of the "miracle." There is poetic and natural, if not explicitly divine, justice in this. But in general, Fellini concentrates on one religion only and on the external features of that religion. "The Waste Land," by contrast, ranges from St. Augustine's arrival at Carthage to the subject of Buddhism, from the stoic resignation of "Death by Water" to the solemn almost hopeful closing chant from the *Upanishads*. Eliot does not mock belief, in this poem, unless in the section on Mme. Sosostris, the fortune telling clairvoyante, yet even this is treated without obvious scorn.

Both "The Waste Land" and *La Dolce Vita* tell a modern story, or better, they reveal modern conditions against an older and supposedly richer background. Fellini draws on Rome's aqueducts, fountains, churches, palaces, monuments, and ruins, and this gives the film a rich, heavy setting, much like Hawthorne's setting for *The*

Marble Faun. Fellini's background is redolent of antiquity, of the Renaissance, of nobler, more spacious and cultured ages piled upon ages. Against this setting, the thinness of modern life appears all the more dramatically. The Steiner episode is typical. The splendid church in which Steiner plays and the flooding organ music of Bach are contrasted with the bare gauze-filled room in which we later see the children Steiner has killed. Inner poverty and outward magnificence form a steady contrast all the way through the film. The episodes in which Sylvia appears contrast the Baths of Caracalla, the Fountain of Trevi, and St. Peter's itself, with the vacuous vivacity of Anita Ekberg, while the party in the aristocratic and decaying villa sets modern enervation in pointed opposition to Renaissance splendor. In "The Waste Land," Eliot has managed a similar effect with different means. The poem is richly suffused with references to and quotations from western and eastern literature of all genres and ages. Passages from the Greeks, Ecclesiastes, Ovid, Augustine, Dante, Shakespeare, Marvell, Kyd, Webster, Spenser, *Tristan and Isolde,* Baudelaire, Verlaine, and Buddha are all worked into the fabric of the poem. The modern moments and experiences of the poem are given depth, significance, and a strange quality of timelessness by Eliot's continual weaving in of the older and more familiar material. In both Fellini's film and Eliot's poem, this background material from the historical and literary past serves to extend the significance of the present, to place the present in some relation to the past, to provide a richness and fullness of texture which the present moment continually lacks, falls short of, or openly mocks.

Fellini and Eliot also share a gift and a taste for witty and elaborate images much like those associated with John Donne and the so-called Metaphysical Poets. And while Fellini's taste runs more to Baroque while Eliot's could be called Mannerist, there is a considerable likeness between say, the opening image of "The Love Song of J. Alfred Prufrock" and the opening image of *La Dolce Vita.* The poem begins:

Let us go then, you and I,
When the evening is spread out against the sky

Like a patient etherised upon a table;
Let us go, through certain half-deserted streets,
The muttering retreats
Of restless nights in one-night cheap hotels
And sawdust restaurants with oyster-shells:
Streets that follow like a tedious argument
Of insidious intent
To lead you to an overwhelming question. . .[7]

The bold and arresting image of the patient, while it startles one, also manages to cast over the entire ensuing poem a sense of illness, paralysis, even narcosis which ends by enveloping the title figure himself. The opening of *La Dolce Vita* also gives us an arresting image which casts its shadow over the whole film.

A vast panorama of the Roman countryside. To one side are the ruins of the San Felice aqueduct, towering arches that come striding across the land. Two thousand years ago, these arches brought water to the city, but now there are many gaps where whole sections of the aqueduct have fallen in. Directly in front is a soccer field, the goal posts dwarfed by the height of the aqueduct. In the distance the sound of motors is heard. A speck in the sky grows rapidly larger. It is a helicopter, and beneath it is a hanging figure. A second helicopter follows close behind. As the 'copters pass over the field the figure suspended below can be clearly seen. A large statue of Christ the Laborer swings from a cable. The shadow of the 'copter and this incongruous figure flashes across the walls of the aqueduct. The helicopters pass on.[8]

This opening shot, besides being quite as witty and as bold as Eliot's image, is also just as complex as the opening of the poem, and its relation to what follows is just as well worked out.

One finds also in the work of both men similar images of innocence. For example, in the opening section of "The Waste Land" there is a quick tender moment of memory:

"You gave me hyacinths first a year ago;
They called me the hyacinth girl."
—Yet when we came back, late, from the Hyacinth garden,
Your arms full, and your hair wet, I could not

Speak, and my eyes failed, I was neither
Living nor dead, and I knew nothing,
Looking into the heart of light, the silence.[9]

This scene is much like the one in which Marcello meets the young girl waiting on table at the empty seaside restaurant, when he experiences a moment of peace, but a moment half marred by the knowledge that it is already too late. Even so, in both poem and film, innocence is a magic moment when things seem a little better, if only for a moment.

And for images of the opposite of innocence both men turn to vague but powerful evocations of the monstrous. Prufrock ruefully speculates, "I should have been a pair of ragged claws/Scuttling across the floors of silent seas." Marcello comes, at the end of *La Dolce Vita,* to the horrible monster the fishermen have caught. Down on the beach, he gazes at the ugly shapeless thing, which with "A lustreless protrusive eye/Stares from the protozoic slime." The lines are from Eliot's "Burbank with a Baedeker: Bleistein with a Cigar," but they describe perfectly the hideous aquatic throwback that lies on the beach and stares at the dawn-exhausted partygoers in the film.[10]

Further, both Eliot and Fellini have hit upon a like way of describing the confusion between the classical and the popular. The distance between classic and jazz is ironically put by Eliot:

O O O O that Shakespeherian Rag—
It's so elegant
So intelligent. . . .[11]

And in *La Dolce Vita,* almost exactly the same technique is used to make the same point when Steiner, sitting down at the great church organ, breaks first into jazz, then into Bach.

One can also find both men concerned and in similar ways with the problem of aging. Prufrock and Guido—the protagonist of *8½* —or Juliet and the title character of "Portrait of a Lady" are close in this respect. These works are also close to one another because they deal with the relations between fantasy and whatever one calls the other part of life. Juliet's world and that of Prufrock, and indeed the whole image-haunted world of "The Waste Land," seem peopled by many of the same figures. There are saints, and barbarians, clowns, monsters, religious and sexual fanatics, apparitions, supported by a rich baroque texture. One thinks of the wildly opulent and sleekly glossy sensuality of the scenes in Susy's villa in *Juliet of the Spirits* and of the opening of Section Two of "The Waste Land":

> *The Chair she sat in, like a burnished throne,*
> *Glowed on the marble, where the glass*
> *Held up by standards wrought with fruited vines*
> *From which a golden Cupidon peeped out. . .*[12]

As one might expect, if the above similarities are not indeed exaggerated beyond usefulness, the endings of some of Eliot's poems are remarkably close to the final sequences of some of Fellini's films. *La Strada* and "The Hollow Men" share a terrible bleakness. "The Love Song of J. Alfred Prufrock" ends with Prufrock's failure becoming apparent just as he has his final and most touching moment of vision.

> *I have heard the mermaids singing, each to each.*
>
> *I do not think that they will sing to me.*
>
> *I have seen them riding seaward on the waves*
> *Combing the white hair of the waves blown back*
> *When the wind blows the water white and black.*
>
> *We have lingered in the chambers of the sea*
> *By sea-girls wreathed with seaweed red and brown*
> *Till human voices wake us, and we drown.*[13]

At the end of *La Dolce Vita,* Marcello wanders down to the beach in the early morning, sees the horrible shapeless one-eyed monster, then becomes aware of the girl from the restaurant, clean, lovely, untouched by the tawdriness of the party, calling to him from across an estuary. They cannot hear one another, and soon Marcello turns away, tugged back into the world he can neither live in nor leave.

Marcello, like Prufrock, can neither reach nor be reached by whatever it is that the girl and the mermaids represent. Both turn back from the sea to drown in human life.

So too in some ways, the ending of "The Waste Land" is rather like the ending of *8½*. Each concludes by remembering and forcing into use what Eliot calls the "fragments I have shored against my ruins." Such as it is, life must be accepted, must indeed be celebrated. So all the figures from Guido's life join in the circle gravely dancing to the brave, tinny music of the little band of circus people, the *saltimbanques* so loved by Picasso and Rilke too, and the night falls; Eliot's poem ends with the stately and circular chanting from the *Upanishads* in a final muted celebration of life ending in the injunction to give, sympathize, and control.

The work of Fellini and Eliot is similar in ways that range from the fortuitous to the important, but beyond particular likenesses of theme, image, tone, or technique, there is, I think, an overriding similarity that has significance not only for their work but for a great deal of twentieth century poetry and film. This crucial similarity I would describe as an aesthetic of disparity. Both Fellini and Eliot have made highly sophisticated, perfectly deliberate attempts to work out a modern narrative form that does not emphasize narrative smoothness or continuity. Each suppresses "links in the chain," each tries to avoid analyzing, giving reasons or explanations. Each is concerned to show, to project an image of modern life as shallow, silly, and sterile, and each uses a technique of juxtaposing images in such a way as to continually insist on disparity without ever saying so in so many words. And indeed, this technique of using simple sequences of images, carefully juxtaposed one against the next in place of a narrative or logical technique, which I have claimed is a technique common to film and modern poetry, is in fact a variety of montage. And montage, whether of pictures or of words, is a technique almost ideally suited to handle the theme of disparity. One image plays against the next, the old can be pushed up against the new, the tender with the harsh, the lovely with the sordid. And as Eliot and Fellini both use the technique, each achieves for his work that overpowering sense of the disparity between what life has been or could be, and what it actually is.

And if this is finally the central theme of the work of both these men, then perhaps their success is in some measure due to the fact that montage provides an excellent form for this subject. Through juxtapositions, Fellini dramatizes the disintegration of modern life against the massive and orderly scenery of Rome, and Eliot shows the triviality of modern life by setting the sordid scenes of the present against the dignity and beauty of a fabric woven of literary reference. Each work is, in its own way, a lament for a nonexistent, or at least, a lost order. Each finds modern life characterized by disparity and lopsidedness, consisting essentially of a "heap of broken images." And the waste land may be, at last, the shadow that lies between the good life and all the endless inequities and disparities, a waste land which Fellini showed in *La Strada* as well as in *La Dolce Vita*, and which Eliot showed in "The Hollow Men" as well as in "The Waste Land."

> *Between the idea*
> *And the reality*
> *Between the motion*
> *And the act*
> *Falls the Shadow. . .*[14]

This sense of disparity, disequilibrium, or unbalance, which I have called the main theme of Eliot's poetry and Fellini's films, is one of the most important ways in which modern art has voiced its troubled awareness of the disorder of our times. And it is significant that the expression of this sense of disorder should be the poetically and filmically formed technique of montage, developed in western countries to emphasize disparity, while its Russian form emphasized conflict.

Thus the sort of montage that one can find in the work of Eliot and Fellini and, of course, in a great many other poems and films, and in other genres and media as well, may be considered one of the most typical and impressive of the ways the modern artist has evolved of looking at his material. Montage as the aesthetic of disparity provides both a way to see one's subject and a way to organize one's work. Properly understood, it may even lend eyes to criticism. For the sort of montage I have been trying to describe is after all a fairly orderly way of coping with the disorders of modern life, and thus may come to be a welcome and powerful force for some sort of viable noncoercive order.

Indeed, the whole problem of order seems to preoccupy us as it has in no period since the Renaissance, when time, mutability, order, degree, and proportion were treated over and over by English writers. The great set pieces on this theme are well known; Elyot's appeal for order, Ulysses' speech on degree in Shakespeare's *Troilus and Cressida*, Thomas Hooker's apostrophe, Spenser's "Mutability Cantos," Shakespeare's sonnets, Donne's anniversaries. This is not the place for another essay on Elizabethan mutability, but it must be mentioned at least, lest we think our own theme newer than it is. Shakespeare's sonnet 15 indeed gives one a sense of the problem as it has always existed, though felt with sudden urgency and strange intensity more by some eras than others.

When I consider everything that grows
Holds in perfection but a little moment,
That this huge stage presenteth nought but shows
Whereon the stars in secret influence comment;
When I perceive that men as plants increase,
Cheered and checked even by the selfsame sky,
Vaunt in their youthful sap, at height decrease,
And wear their brave state out of memory;
Then the conceit of this inconstant stay
Sets you most rich in youth before my sight,
Where wasteful Time debateth with Decay
To change your day of youth to sullied night;
And, all in war with Time for love of you,
As he takes from you, I ingraft you new.

The great universal order is hidden, the stars make *secret* and obscure comment. On earth, order seems to reach no higher than the seasonal order of birth, growth, height, decline, and death; and this order of natural process is an order that undoes beauty, like Frost's malevolent design. Innumerable readers have felt the weakness of the ending of many of Shakespeare's sonnets. The one just quoted, for example, ends in sheer assertion. What time takes away the poet says he will supply. He cannot of course, at least not in most senses, but he feels impelled to protest and this says all that he can say. To be human is to oppose the descent to ruin and death. As Unamuno once put it, "If it is nothingness that awaits us, let us make an injustice of it."[15]

Twentieth century consciousness of this problem has by now created almost as great a statement of the dilemma of order as that left by the Renaissance. One can find, for example, a ringing statement of it in Alfred North Whitehead's *The Function of Reason.* "History discloses two main tendencies in the course of events. One tendency is exemplified in the slow decay of physical nature. With stealthy inevitableness, there is degradation of energy. The sources of activity sink downward and downward. Their very matter wastes. The other tendency is exemplified by the yearly renewal of nature in the spring, and by the upward course of biological evolution. Reason is the self-discipline of the originative element in history. Apart from the operations of Reason, this element is anarchic."[16]

And Nathanael West's *Miss Lonelyhearts* has a brilliant description of entropy as it commonly appears. "Man has a tropism for order. Keys in one pocket, change in another. Mandolins are tuned G D A E. The physical world has a tropism for disorder, entropy. Man against nature . . . the battle of the centuries. Keys yearn to mix with change, Mandolins strive to get out of tune. Every order has within it the germ of destruction. All order is doomed, yet the battle is worthwhile."[17] It is this kind of awareness that produces the "heap of broken images," the world Yeats complained of, saying, "The best lack all conviction, while the worst are full of passionate intensity." Dadaism and films like *Un Chien Andalou* reflect a similar vision. And indeed it sometimes seems as though there were abroad a sinister entropic power. When a great work like the *Cantos* of Ezra Pound or *The Bridge* of Hart Crane, work designed specifically to close gaps, make connections, join the past and the future, can be sabotaged from within, as it were, can fail to achieve enough order to present the theme of order, and can end as formless ruins though designed as monuments to order, one wonders less that insanity or suicide can cap the effort.

But it has never been an easy problem. Spenser never finished the "Mutability Cantos" either. And we are, with good reason, fiercely on guard against phony order and oppressive order. As E. M. Forster has observed, "In the world of daily life, the world we perforce inhabit, there is much talk about order, particularly from statesmen and politicians. They tend, however, to confuse order with orders, just as they confuse creation with regulations. Order, I suggest, is something evolved from within, not something imposed from without; it is an internal stability, a vital harmony, and in the social and political category it has never existed except for the convenience of historians."[18] And there are in art many phony orders, such as the totally rational world of the detective novel, or the neat formulaic characters and ritual plots in a run of the mill Hollywood comedy. As one of Nathanael West's heroes snarls at his tidy girl friend, "your order is meaningless, my chaos is significant." Perhaps significant chaos is a good generic description for such poems as Yeats' "Second Coming," for Dali's limp watch and landscape paintings, the Resnais-Robbe-Grillet *Last Year at Marienbad,* and indeed, a great deal of contemporary artistic expression.

9 / The Survival of Humanism

IN 1923 BÉLA BALÁZS NOTED THAT "THE DISCOVERY of printing gradually rendered illegible the faces of men." He went on to describe the effects of the film on society in terms that have been widely quoted and imitated:

> Now the film is about to inaugurate a new direction in our culture. Many million people sit in the picture houses every evening and purely through vision, experience happenings, characters, emotions, moods, even thoughts, without the need for many words. For words do not touch the spiritual content of the pictures and are merely passing instruments of as yet undeveloped forms of art. Humanity is already learning the rich and colourful language of gesture, movement and facial expression. This is not a language of signs as a substitute for words, like the sign-language of the deaf-and-dumb—it is the visual means of communication, without intermediary, of souls clothed in flesh. Man has again become visible.[1]

But the vast and impressive visual resources of the film and the obvious importance of the new form did not blind Balázs to the function of literature nor did it lead him to a silly or thoughtless dismissal of words as useless or old fashioned. The essential sanity which underlies and gives sinew to Balázs' critical brilliance led him to insist in a clear and explicit manner that the purely visual should not and in fact did not in any sense replace verbal culture.

> For it is not the same spirit, not the same soul that is expressed once in words and once in gestures. Music does not express the same thing as poetry in a different way—it expresses something quite different. When we dip the bucket of words in the depths, we bring up other things than when we do the same with gestures. But let no one think that I want to bring back the culture of movement and gesture in place of the culture of words, for neither can be a substitute for the other. Without a rational, conceptual culture and the scientific development that goes with it there can be no social and hence no human progress. The connecting tissue of modern society is the word spoken and written, without which all organization and planning would be impossible. On the other hand fascism has shown us where the tendency to reduce human culture to subconscious emotions in place of clear concepts would lead humanity.

Lest this be thought a purely political comment, Balázs quickly insists that "what I am talking about is only art, and even here there is no question of displacing the more rational art of the word."[2]

A sobering example of the film's possibilities for powerful irrational political appeal is Leni Riefenstahl's *The Triumph of the Will*, the well-known documentary which extols Hitler and Naziism with appalling visual lyricism. And it is significant that the finest film yet to appear in condemnation of Naziism, Alain Resnais's *Night and Fog*, is a sober and literary film, very restrained and low-keyed in its visual images, while enormous importance is given by Resnais to Jean Cayrol's moving verbal commentary. The narration is in fact the basis or center of the film, and as the visual aspect is rigorously subordinated to the literary aspect, we can see how Resnais tries to make the film of reason rise against the politics of unreason. And as long as this much sanity remains, there can be no question of the image replacing the word, or of visual media replacing books, or any of the other claims currently made by the media specialists. We shall need both words and images—not because it makes a comfortable compromise, but because words and images have separate but indispensable functions.

George Steiner has said, with admirable clarity and directness, that the two principal functions of language are "the conveyance of humane order which we call law, and the communication of the quick of the human spirit which we call grace."[3] Now I think it can be argued that insofar as film is a kind of language, it is at present the language best fitted to convey that "quick of the human spirit" of which Mr. Steiner speaks, while modern poetry has shown itself better suited to the "conveyance of humane order." Put another way, it is to modern poetry that we must look for current formulations of and ideas about order, while it is to the film that we have come to look for the actual image of man.

Indeed poetry is almost by its very nature concerned with order. As Paul Fussell has put it recently in his book on *Poetic Meter and Poetic Form*, "Civilization is an impulse toward order; but high civilizations are those which operate from a base of order without at the same time denying the claims of the unpredictable and even the irrational. The impulse toward the metrical organization of assertions seems to partake of the more inclusive human impulse toward order."[4] But simple orderliness is not, of course, enough. And in its striving for a humane sort of order, an order sufficiently humane to be acceptable as law, poetry in this century has been quite explicit in its rejection of false orders, patterns, masks, rules, rigidities, and constrictions in general.

So Yeats describes in "The Circus Animals' Desertion" how all his earlier patterns, projects, masks, and systems each led finally nowhere. Each was a "ladder," a temporary aid, an artificial order adapted to gain some poetic end, but they all failed because, Yeats seems to say, they had more system than humanness to them. So the poem ends:

> *Those masterful images because complete*
> *Grew in pure mind, but out of what began?*
> *A mound of refuse or the sweepings of a street,*
> *Old kettles, old bottles, and a broken can,*
> *Old iron, old bones, old rags, that raving slut*
> *Who keeps the till. Now that my ladder's gone,*

I must lie down where all the ladders start,
In the foul rag-and-bone shop of the heart.[5]

The result of the voyage is to come back to the beginning, and the beginning is always the unadorned and unaccommodated human being. Edwin Muir has said it too, in his "The Journey Back," "so I hie me back/To my sole starting-point, my random self/That in these rags and tatters clothes the soul."[6] Yeats' poem goes no further than this starting point, and though it is filled with an elegiac sense of loss, we see Yeats arriving at the realization that no artificial or imposed order can work; that if there is to be order or meaning, it will have to be human, with all that that implies. Form alone had failed him every time.

Ezra Pound, in a passage singled out for praise by F. O. Matthiessen, has also written movingly about what we will need to save and what dismantle before we can arrive at a true order.

What thou lovest well remains,
the rest is dross
What thou lovs't well shall not be reft from thee
What thou lovs't well is thy true heritage
Whose world, or mine or theirs
or is it of none?

First came the seen, then thus the palpable
Elysium, though it were in the halls of hell,
What thou lovs't well is thy true heritage

The ant's a centaur in his dragon world.
Pull down thy vanity, it is not man
Made courage, or made order, or made grace, . . .

This is not an appeal to a deity; it is instead a dignified, if a little old fashioned, appeal to the order of nature, for Pound goes on to advise us to "Learn of the green world what can be thy place/In scaled invention or true artistry."[7]

Perhaps the problem posed by the false or limited sort of order is best put by T. S. Eliot, who writes in "East Coker":

. . . There is, it seems to us,
At best, only a limited value
In the knowledge derived from experience.
The knowledge imposes a pattern, and falsifies,
For the pattern is new in every moment
And every moment is a new and shocking
Valuation of all we have been.[8]

Modern poetry can be thought of as a long continuous sequence of these "new and shocking valuations" and occasionally a poet or a poem has gone on beyond the function of poetry Robert Frost suggested when he spoke of poetry as "a momentary stay against confusion," to pose a new, humane, and hopefully livable sort of order. Wallace Stevens took humane order as his central theme, and one of the best known expressions of it is his "The Idea of Order at Key West." The poem is about Stevens' vision of a woman singing by the sea, and about his perception that the woman, in singing—a metaphor for poetry or art generally—is the sole maker of her world and the sole source of order for her world.

It was her voice that made
The sky acutest at its vanishing.
She measured to the hour its solitude.
She was the single artificer of the world
In which she sang. And when she sang, the sea,
Whatever self it had, became the self
That was her song, for she was the maker. Then we,
As we beheld her striding there alone,
Knew that there never was a world for her
Except the one she sang and, singing, made.

The poem closes with a final note of triumph in having recognized:

The maker's rage to order words of the sea,
Words of the fragrant portals, dimly-starred,
And of ourselves and of our origins,
In ghostlier demarcations, keener sounds.[9]

Order in this poem, as elsewhere in Stevens' work, is not external, not inherent in things. It is the ordering power of the mind, the order inherent in the imagination and most visible in the artist. Such order as there is, is a human order, which is projected upon the outer world, or turned to despite the outer world. The beginning and the end of order is human. Again, it is perhaps the poetry of Eliot, richer, more various, and more alive with simple human emotion than that of Stevens, that contains the fullest modern examination of the idea of order. For instance, in "Burnt Norton," while he provides no logical argument for order, and indulges in no imperative demands that his special vision of order be imposed, he describes instead the sort of inner calm that seems worth calling a humane order.

Time and the bell have buried the day,
The black cloud carries the sun away.
Will the sunflower turn to us, will the clematis
Stray down, bend to us; tendril and spray
Clutch and cling?
Chill
Fingers of yew be curled
Down on us? After the kingfisher's wing
Has answered light to light, and is silent, the light is still
At the still point of the turning world.[10]

Eliot perceives, I think, a heart of still light as if in answer to the heart of clamorous darkness that has been so often described since Conrad. What this heart of light means, or is exactly, is not easy to say, but as Eliot apprehends it, "Only by the form, the patterns/Can words or music reach/the stillness, as a Chinese jar still/Moves perpetually in its stillness."[11] And we are reminded of the sort of ordered permanence Keats perceived in the Grecian urn. *Four Quartets* is, of course, one of the great modern poems of order. The theme is everywhere in them and random quotation can hardly suggest the power with which Eliot invests his sense that, at last, beneath the bewildering complexity of life, there can be found or made a fairly simple, humanly satisfactory order. The end of "Little

Gidding," in its quietness, its relatively uniform meter, its urge to reconcile and unite rather than juxtapose and divide, may serve to suggest Eliot's sense of the sort of order than can still be reached:

We shall not cease from exploration
And the end of all our exploring
Will be to arrive where we started
And know the place for the first time.
Through the unknown, remembered gate
When the last of earth left to discover
Is that which was the beginning;
At the source of the longest river
The voice of the hidden waterfall
And the children in the apple-tree
Not known, because not looked for
But heard, half-heard, in the stillness
Between two waves of the sea.
Quick now, here, now, always—
A condition of complete simplicity
(Costing not less than everything)
And all shall be well and
All manner of thing shall be well
When the tongues of flame are in-folded
Into the crowned knot of fire
And the fire and the rose are one.[12]

Eliot and Stevens are perhaps the most eloquent in their insistence that it is the human imagination which has the greatest power to order experience and unify life, but it is a theme common to much recent poetry, a theme which has even received extensive critical and analytical description in the work of Northrop Frye and others. But, splendid as this statement of order has been, poetry has shown comparatively little interest in the actual human shape of the ordered life. That is to say, while fine poems have been written about order and about grace as well, there is rarely a solid human presence in a modern poem. Few recent poems center on a fully revealed, recognizably human figure; there are few great persons or characters to be found or who are remembered from modern poems.

Robert Frost—the most old fashioned of currently praised poets—has been most successful at this. Mary and Silas in "The Death of the Hired Man," the Hill Wife from the poem of that name, and many other poems of Frost's have a real human presence at the center. But Eliot's Prufrock is the nearest to an adequately presented human figure in Eliot's work, and the figure in Yeats' "Among School Children" is the closest Yeats came. Auden's poems on Freud and Yeats start with actual men as subjects, but the men become more and more representatives of ideas or approaches as the poems proceed. In *Paterson,* William Carlos Williams has a central character, but he is an abstraction, he is the city personified. Stevens' "Sunday Morning" and Robert Lowell's "Quaker Graveyard in Nantucket" are two other poems which work out from a central human figure, but in none of these poems is there as strong, as full, as insistent a human presence as in most of our great movies.

If poetry has had to struggle to invest its visions of order with a human aspect, film has had almost the opposite problem, that of how to invest its images of man with some sort of significant order. If poetry has had trouble evoking the human figure, film has had the human figure since the start: the question has been what to do with it. It is fascinating in this connection to note, as Balázs has reminded us, that the movies' first great achievement antedated the discovery and development of what we now think of as film form or film language. Silent comedy of the sort Chaplin did so well doesn't depend on editing or montage at all, yet slapstick and Chaplinesque humor is pure film, very funny and still vital. As I have suggested, this may be because it is about man and the mechanical modern world or man and the inanimate world. In its own way, then, even the earliest achievements of the film focused instinctively, as it were, on the condition of being human. A later reminder of the strength of the unelaborated human image might be found in W. C. Fields' movies. His films normally suffer from weak and silly plots, terrible photography, incompetent direction, sloppy editing, and embarrassing co-stars, yet such films as *You Can't Cheat an Honest Man* and *Never Give a Sucker an Even Break* are splendid, if only because Fields' screen presence is so arresting, so authentic, and so funny. Half Falstaff, half Sancho Panza, Fields raises the sardonic, inept blusterer to epic but still human proportions, and his unquenchable self simply dwarfs everything else in sight.

Despite flurries of enthusiasm for abstraction, surrealism, landscapes, and tone poems, the film, virtually alone of modern visual arts, has taken the human image as its subject. Further, the film has tended to insist that the importance of anything is as it affects people. To the old claims of humanism it has brought new material and new urgency. Thus Balázs could claim that "everything that happens, happens in the last resort to men and through men. You want to show a great civilization, great technical progress? Show them in the men who work; show their faces, their eyes, and then we shall be able to tell what the civilization means and what it is worth. You want to show the harvest of the fields? Only the ploughman's face will lend expression to the face of the earth."[13]

Perhaps man is no longer the measure of all things, but man remains the measure of the world on film. Cesare Zavattini writes that "the cinema's overwhelming desire to see, to analyze, its hunger for reality, is an act of concrete homage towards other people," and Stanley Kauffmann has defended the increasingly open treatment of sexuality in the films—as he might have defended a great many more things about them—because in its honest and often joyful way it emphasizes the "desirability of being human, even with all the trouble it involves."[14] The films of Jean Renoir, for example, show just this emphasis on the desirability of being human; it is the main theme of *The Grand Illusion* and of other films. And this too is perhaps the secret behind the enormous appeal of the James Dean films *Rebel Without a Cause* and, in particular, *East of Eden,* since Dean managed to avoid the easy stereotypes of adolescence to bring into sight the real quality of youth. So too, a film such as Claude Lelouch's *A Man and a Woman,* while not much admired by cinema intellectuals because it is thematically lightweight, has nevertheless a steady if not a very deep or troubled sense of simple and simply attractive humanness.

Nor need we confine this quality to happy or to neutral films. Many movies that are very close to classical tragedy, such as *Rocco and His Brothers* and *La Strada,* also insist on the need, not just the desirability, of being human. *Rocco* pits family values against city life, personal values against imposed values, yet is honest enough not to falsify the outcome. *La Strada,* revolving around three people whom psychology would call abnormal, nevertheless manages to find and then insist on humanness in the animal Zampano, in the half-wit Gelsomina, and in the Fool. The film has the pace and power of a Greek tragedy; its theme, like that of Sophocles' *Ajax,* might be said to be an examination of what it is to be human. In these films and in many others, we must, I think, agree with Parker Tyler's summary of the film's achievement. "Photography," Tyler writes, "*revived* the classic human image . . . because photography began to move: became the *movies.* Suddenly man's representational image was galvanized, and in this sense human identity in art was given a new meaning through its additional element: kinesis."[15]

The human image does indeed dominate the movies; the movies are still fundamentally representational. This may or may not justify calling them classical, but the film's allegiance to what is human goes continually beyond simple representationalism, just as the human image, by any reasonable definition of that phrase, must mean more than mere hominoid appearance. At their best, film makers have tried to reach beyond the so easily available surfaces of things and people, to reach as literature has had to reach, for the internal qualities of men. Thus Carl Dreyer could claim that if the film maker "confines himself to the soulless impersonal photography of what his eyes can perceive, he has no style."[16] The camera eye is just as interpretive as the novelist's eye. It is evasion to shuffle it off and talk about the documentation of things as they are, or as they appear. Any film maker selects and edits reality; he may choose to do the selecting and the editing in such a way as to bring out or insist on simple human values, as De Sica did in *The Bicycle Thief,* or the selection and editing may be soulless, impersonal, and inhuman by selecting for titillation, violence, prurience, and glamor.

Apart from the creative intelligence which edits it, the raw material of a film is no more impressive and no more significant than the material of any other art. So Pudovkin could say that "editing is the basic creative force, by power of which the soulless photographs (the separate shots) are engineered into living, cinematographic form."[17] Anyone who has seen unedited Eisenstein footage and a finished Eisenstein film will know at once what Pudovkin means. Eisenstein's Mexican footage, now in the Museum of Modern Art in New York, is, in its present form, meaningless, blank, without much more than formal and scholarly interest. Had he finished the film, the same material would have had, without doubt, immense human significance.

To Dreyer and Pudovkin must be added, one final time, Vachel Lindsay, who said of his *The Art of the Moving Picture*, "this book is a struggle against the non-humanness of the undisciplined photograph."[18] Like Dreyer and Pudovkin, Lindsay insists that raw photography is soulless, impersonal, and somehow inhuman, apart from the creative ordering of the film maker. At its simplest, this means that the unedited shots of a film are without much life, interest, or meaning until they have been pieced together in the proper sequence. But beyond this, the passionate quality of the three utterances just quoted suggest that the statements are really aimed at the flood of movies which manage to betray the human being and the image of humanness into stereotype and mannerism, into glamor and falseness, into emotional dishonesty, or which manage to deliver us over to our destructive instincts for aggression and violence. Whether it is the average television commercial, the average spectacle or bedroom farce, the average experimental film, or a film well conceived but misedited by its producers as so many of Welles' have been, or whether it is films of joyous Naziism like *The Triumph of the Will*, there is always a chance that sleazy or inhuman motives, whether conscious or not, will creep in and poison the end result. Nor is this a matter mainly of moralizing, except insofar as Matthew Arnold was right in saying that that is moral which teaches us how to live, and Whitehead was right in saying that "style is the ultimate morality of mind." The problem is one of style, and style has always involved some sort of ordering process.

The problem of the film has indeed always been just how to draw from its rich and varied human material an order that is significant and satisfying without imposing on that material an orderliness that will be oppressive and stultifying. Too much formalizing and one gets the dead and "soulless" sort of image that *Last Year at Marienbad* produced. Orson Welles remarked of the film that it reminded him of *Vogue*, and it is true that in that film, posed, posturing, unmoved, and unmoving figurines are substituted for real human beings, a fact that was not lost on the majority of viewers.

Thus it appears that the humanness of the films and their sense of order are inextricably bound up together, and I would argue that many of the great films that have been made so far are films in which both humanness and order are included or reconciled or respected, in which humanness and order are in some way seen to be compatible.

Ingmar Bergman's *The Seventh Seal* explores a chaotic and disintegrating world through the eyes of the knight who is the central figure. He is a simple man with simple and clear virtues—loyal, courageous, a seeker, just and steadfast. Insofar as he is a believable figure, we perceive, with him, just how chaotic the surrounding world is. So with Fellini's *8½*, a rambling film about a film maker's search for his subject, which he thinks out as he goes along and which indeed quite accurately reflects the way Fellini actually made *8½*. The thing that unites this movie is the presence of the hero, and the final scene, which formally pulls the movie together, is not a trick or a gimmick but the hero's natural last move. He brings a measure of order to his film, and to his life, by means of a great and sweeping impulse to accept. Thus he accepts all of the past, all of his friends and enemies, all of his life, and all the figures from this life join hands and dance slowly and gravely around in a circle as the light fails, while a simple little tune, heard through the growing darkness, holds out against that darkness. Thus, if the ending of this film works, it is not because it is a new idea or a subtle philosophical statement, nor is it the expected last piece in a design; it is the simple human gesture that a man such as Guido would perhaps make in real life.

Modern poetry, as has been noted, has tended rather strongly toward the abstract and the philosophical. But the film, though it shares some of the ideas and some of the techniques of modern poetry, is not, as a medium, well adapted to expressing abstract ideas or carrying on philosophical dialogue. Thus it has been virtually forced to embody its ideas in specific human figures. So a film such as *L'Avventura*, while it relentlessly explores the hollowness of modern life and love, does not end with despair or chaos, because through all the trials, the long and lingering frustrations and futilities recorded in the film, the central figure, Claudia, comes to have a remarkable and unshakable integrity, and it is her simple human integrity, her faithfulness to herself, that emerges, not so much as the idea of order, but as the image of order, in *L'Avventura*.

Agnes Varda's splendid but not widely known *Cleo from 5 to 7* will furnish a final example. The film concerns a young Parisian *chanteuse*, whose life at the start of the film is vapid, cluttered, artificial, chaotic, and unhappy beneath its extravagant surface gaiety. However, upon learning that she is ill and probably soon to die, Cleo gradually decides to *live* the rest of her life, and the sentence of death marks the start of her emergence as a woman; she becomes warm, real, and even happy. It is her own inner resources that come to her rescue, revive her, and force order upon the hectic superficial activity of her life. The film opens with an old woman telling Cleo's fortune with a Tarot deck—she predicts death. The film ends, though, predicting life, with a love scene in a city park; and these two sequences mark the poles of the theme. Chance, bustle, and chaos are death, while inner calm, love, and control are life. Eliot's "The Waste Land" ends with the advice that we need to learn to give, to sympathize, and to control; W. H. Auden has said "we must love one another or die." *Cleo from 5 to 7* does not say these things, it shows them, acts them out, embodies them, in a real and believable woman.

These films and a great many others deal with order and disorder in completely human terms. And it is not just that modern poetry has a tendency toward the speculative, while the film, by its nature, insists more on people. In the films I have mentioned, it also seems that the film makers have been more actively aware and more successful in making the point that for twentieth century man, with his immense knowledge and in his immensely rapid and confusing world, significant order must be a human order. Order is no longer to be found in religious formulations, in the order of nature, in the design of the heavens, in science or in history; it is not in social order or orderliness, not in codes, mores, and laws; order for us, as these films have provided images of it, is a kind of fidelity to one's best self, a quality that may be seen in the knight and the clown in *The Seventh Seal*, in Claudia in *L'Avventura*, in Guido of *8½*, in Cleo of *Cleo from 5 to 7*. Order is what makes their lives cohere in defiance of all the external impulses to chaos.

One could list many more examples of modern films which are firmly centered on human figures and in which the theme is the identification of what is human: Truffaut's Charlie in *Shoot the Piano Player*, the boy in his *The 400 Blows*, Diego in Resnais's *La Guerre est Finie*, the married couple in Antonioni's *La Notte*, the spinster and the river bum in *The African Queen*, and so on. But the point would remain the same; that the films have done more than any other art to keep intact the image of man as a being whose full humanity depends somehow on his being self-ordered. Indeed the film has come the closest of modern arts to fulfilling Alexis de Tocqueville's conviction as he wrote, "I am persuaded that in the end democracy diverts the imagination from all that is external to man, and fixes it on man alone."[19]

Modern literature has been pursuing this aim, as has the film, and if literature now abounds with brilliant and moving arguments for humane order and human grace, the film is supplying the complementary vision of visible order and visible grace. And it has taken the combined efforts of modern poetry and film to show us that when we find an order that is useful and livable, that order will have a human face.

Selected Bibliography

THE FOLLOWING IS A HIGHLY SELECTIVE LIST OF BOOKS AND ESSAYS *which bear immediately upon film and literature. No attempt has been made to list works which deal exclusively with film theory or with literary theory. Further materials for the study of literature and film may be found in the notes to the present volume and in the admirable bibliography in Nicoll's* Film and Theatre.

Agee, James. *Agee on Film*, 2 vols., Boston, Beacon Press, 1964.

Armes, Roy. *French Cinema Since 1946*, 2 vols., London, Zwemmer, 1966.

Arnheim, Rudolf. *Film as Art*, Berkeley and Los Angeles, University of California Press, 1960.

Balázs, Béla. *Theory of the Film*, New York, Roy, 1955.

Bazin, André. *What Is Cinema*, Berkeley and Los Angeles, University of California Press, 1967.

Bergman, Ingmar. *Four Screenplays of Ingmar Bergman*, New York, Simon and Schuster, 1960.

Bluestone, George. *Novels into Film*, Baltimore, Johns Hopkins Press, 1957.

Cocteau, Jean. *Cocteau on the Film*, New York, Roy, 1954.

Eisenstein, Sergei. *Film Form*, New York, Harcourt, Brace, 1949.

———. *The Film Sense*, New York, Harcourt, Brace, 1942.

Fenollosa, Ernest. *The Chinese Written Character as a Medium for Poetry*, London, Stanley Nott, 1936.
Frank, Joseph. *The Widening Gyre*, New Brunswick, N. J., Rutgers University Press, 1963.
Geduld, Harry M. *Film Makers on Film Making*, Bloomington and London, Indiana University Press, 1967.
Hauser, Arnold. *The Social History of Art*, 2 vols., New York, Knopf, 1951.
Kauffmann, Stanley. *A World on Film*, New York, Harper and Row, 1966.
Lindsay, Vachel. *The Art of the Moving Picture*, New York, Macmillan, 1915.
MacCann, Richard Dyer, ed. *Film: A Montage of Theories*, New York, Dutton, 1966.
Mann, Thomas. "On the Film," in *Past Masters and Other Papers*, New York, Knopf, 1933.
Nicoll, Allardyce. *Film and Theatre*, New York, Crowell, 1936.
Panofsky, Erwin. "Style and Medium in the Moving Pictures," *Bulletin of the Department of Art and Archaeology*, Princeton University, 1934, reprinted in *Film: An Anthology*, ed. Daniel Talbot, Berkeley and Los Angeles, University of California Press, 1959.
Pudovkin, V. I. *Film Technique and Film Acting*, London, Vision: Mayflower, 1958.
Read, Sir Herbert. "The Poet and the Film," in *A Coat of Many Colours*, London, Routledge and Kegan Paul, 1945.
Sheridan, Marion C., et al. *The Motion Picture and the Teaching of English*, New York, Appleton-Century-Crofts, 1965.
Steiner, George. *Language and Silence*, New York, Atheneum, 1967.
Tyler, Parker. *The Three Faces of the Film*, New York, Yoseloff, 1960.
Wilbur, Richard. "A Poet and the Movies," in W. R. Robinson, *Man and the Movies*, Baton Rouge, Louisiana State University Press, 1967.
Woolf, Virginia. "The Movies and Reality," *The New Republic*, XLVII, August 4, 1926.

Notes

1 / Literature and Film

1. Quoted in Henry Adams, *Mont-Saint-Michel and Chartres*, Boston, Houghton Mifflin, 1904, pp. 64–65.

2. Kenneth Clark, "The Blot and the Diagram," *Encounter*, No. 112, January 1963, p. 31.

3. Arnold Hauser, *The Social History of Art*, Vol. 2, New York, Knopf, 1951, p. 956.

4. James Agee, "Comedy's Greatest Era," in *Agee on Film: Reviews and Comments*, Boston, Beacon Press, pp. 15–16.

5. Ingmar Bergman, *Four Screenplays of Ingmar Bergman*, New York, Simon and Schuster, 1960, pp. xxi–xxii.

6. Hauser, p. 947.

7. Erwin Panofsky, "Style and Medium in the Moving Pictures," *Bulletin of the Department of Art and Archaeology*, Princeton University, 1934, reprinted in *Film: An Anthology*, ed. Daniel Talbot, Berkeley and Los Angeles, University of California Press, 1959, pp. 15–32.

8. Sergei Eisenstein, *Film Form*, Cleveland and New York, World (Meridian), 1957, pp. 232–233.

9. E. H. Gombrich, *Meditations on a Hobby Horse*, London, Phaidon, 1963, p. 87, and Roy Armes, *French Cinema Since 1946*, Vol. 1, London, Zwemmer, 1966, p. 7.

10. Sir Herbert Read, *A Coat of Many Colours*, London, Routledge and Kegan Paul, 1945, pp. 230–231.
11. George Steiner, *Language and Silence*, New York, Atheneum, 1967, p. 101.
12. Quoted in Jay Leyda, *Kino*, London, George Allen and Unwin, 1960, p. 130.
13. Quoted in Armes, Vol. 2, p. 95.
14. Read, p. 230.
15. Stanley Kauffmann, *A World on Film*, New York, Harper and Row, 1966, p. 421.
16. Quoted in Armes, Vol. 2, pp. 84–89.
17. Jean Cocteau, *Cocteau on the Film*, a conversation recorded by André Fraigneau, trans. Vera Traill, New York, Roy Publishers, Inc., 1954, p. 101.

2 / LITERARY ORIGINS AND BACKGROUNDS OF THE FILMS

1. Sergei Eisenstein, *Film Form*, Cleveland & New York, World (Meridian), 1957, pp. 200, 205, 208, 216, 217, and 213.
2. Ibid., p. 213.
3. Joseph Frank, *The Widening Gyre*, New Brunswick, N. J., Rutgers University Press, 1963, pp. 14–16.
4. Thomas Hardy, *The Dynasts*, Pts. I and II, London, Macmillan, 1948, pp. x, 216.
5. Walt Whitman, *The Early Poems and the Fiction*, New York, New York University Press, 1963, pp. 34, 38, 40.
6. Walt Whitman, *Leaves of Grass*, The First (1855) Edition, New York, Viking, 1961, pp. 31, 37, 25.
7. Ibid., p. 24.
8. Whitman, *Leaves of Grass*, ed. Blodgett and Bradley, New York, New York University Press, 1965, p. 300.
9. Arthur Rimbaud, *Poèmes*, Paris, Gallimard, 1960, p. 130.
10. Walter Pater, *The Renaissance* (First Edition 1873), New York, Macmillan, 1905, p. 130.
11. See Ernest Fenollosa, *The Chinese Written Character as a Medium for Poetry*, London, Stanley Nott, 1936.
12. Vachel Lindsay, *The Art of the Moving Picture*, New York, Macmillan, 1915, pp. 171, 185.

3 / Griffith and Eisenstein: The Uses of Literature in Film

1. Rudolph Arnheim, *Film*, London, Faber, 1933. See the section called "Film and Reality" in the volume called *Film as Art* published by the University of California Press in 1960.

2. Béla Balázs, *Theory of the Film*, London, Dennis Dobson, 1953, p. 31.

3. V. I. Pudovkin, *Film Technique and Film Acting*, Trans. Ivor Montagu, London, Vision: Mayflower, 1958, pp. 23–24.

4. Griffith's play, called A *Fool and a Girl*, was given at the Columbia Theatre, Washington, D. C., in 1907.

5. Vachel Lindsay, *The Art of the Moving Picture*, New York, Macmillan, 1915, pp. 65–66.

6. It should be noted that Griffith's intercutting of stories separated in space and time was anticipated by Edwin S. Porter in *The Kleptomaniac* in 1905.

7. Sergei Eisenstein, *The Film Sense*, Cleveland and New York, World (Meridian), 1957, p. 2.

8. Ibid., p. 4.

9. Quoted in ibid., p. 6.

10. Ibid., p. 13.

11. Ibid., p. 20.

12. Ibid., pp. 25–26.

13. Ibid., pp. 29–30.

14. Quoted in ibid., p. 47.

15. Ibid., p. 49.

16. Ibid., p. 53.

17. Ibid., p. 56.

18. Ibid., pp. 58, 61–62.

19. Quoted in Roy Armes, *French Cinema Since 1946*, Vol. 2, London, Zwemmer, 1966, p. 109.

4 / Literary Technique and Film Technique

1. Michelangelo Antonioni, *Screenplays of Michelangelo Antonioni*, trans. Louis Brigante and Roger J. Moore, New York, Orion, 1963, p. 357.

2. King James Version, Ecclesiastes 12:1–4.

3. Ovid, *The Metamorphoses*, trans. A. E. Watts, Berkeley and Los Angeles, University of California Press, 1954, p. 108.

4. John Keats, *The Poetical Works of John Keats*, Second Edition, ed. H. W. Garrod, Oxford, Clarendon Press, 1958, p. 458.

5. Vachel Lindsay, *The Art of the Moving Picture*, New York, Macmillan, 1915, p. 54.

6. Geoffrey Chaucer, *The Works of Geoffrey Chaucer*, ed. F. N. Robinson, Boston, Houghton Mifflin, 1957, p. 161.

7. *The Renaissance in England*, ed. Rollins and Baker, Boston, Heath, 1954, p. 78.

8. C. S. Lewis, *English Literature in the Sixteenth Century*, Oxford, Clarendon Press, 1954, pp. 136–139.

9. Nathaniel Hawthorne, *The Marble Faun*, Boston and New York, Houghton Mifflin, 1897, Riverside Edition, pp. 196, 360.

10. Ibid., pp. 58, 61, 62, 63, 65.

11. Mark Twain, *Huckleberry Finn*, New York, Norton, 1961, p. 96.

12. James Agee, *A Death in the Family*, New York, McDowell Obolensky, 1957, p. 81.

13. Ibid., pp. 4–5.

14. "The Bishop Orders His Tomb at Saint Praxeds Church," ll. 1–9, in *The Shorter Poems of Robert Browning*, ed. W. C. De Vane, New York, Appleton-Century-Crofts, 1934, pp. 54–55.

15. William Shakespeare, *King Lear*, Baltimore, Penguin Books, 1958, pp. 67–68.

5 / VERBAL AND VISUAL LANGUAGES

1. Christopher Marlowe, *Doctor Faustus*, ed. J. D. Jump, Cambridge, Mass., Harvard University Press, 1962, p. 92.

2. V. I. Pudovkin, *Film Technique and Film Acting*, trans. Ivor Montagu, London, Vision: Mayflower, 1958, p. 27.

3. William Shakespeare, *Measure for Measure*, Baltimore, Penguin Books, 1956, p. 72.

4. Rudolf Arnheim, *Film As Art*, Berkeley and Los Angeles, University of California Press, 1957, p. 15.

5. See the title essay in E. H. Gombrich's *Meditations on a Hobby Horse*, London, Phaidon, 1963.

6. Ogden Nash, *Verses from 1929 On*, Boston and Toronto, Little, Brown, 1959, p. 239.

7. Lawrence Durrell, *Justine*, New York, Pocket Books, p. 199.

8. *Shakespeare's Sonnets,* ed. H. E. Rollins, New York, Appleton-Century-Crofts, p. 55.

9. J. D. Salinger, "A Perfect Day for Bananafish," in *Nine Stories,* New York, New American Library, 1954, p. 7.

10. Thomas Aquinas, from the *Summa Theologica,* Q. 85, Art 7, in *Introduction to St. Thomas Aquinas,* New York, Random House, 1948, p. 419.

11. John Donne, *Devotions Upon Emergent Occasions,* Cambridge, Cambridge University Press, 1923, p. 98.

12. Sergei Eisenstein, *The Film Sense,* Cleveland and New York, World (Meridian), 1957, p. 234.

13. Roy Armes, *French Cinema Since 1946,* Vol. 2, London, Zwemmer, 1966, p. 18.

6 / Film and Modern Fiction

1. Luigi Pirandello, *Shoot!; The Notebooks of Serafino Gubbio, Cinematograph Operator,* New York, E. P. Dutton, 1926, p. 10.

2. F. Scott Fitzgerald, *The Last Tycoon,* New York, Scribners, 1941, p. 20.

3. John Dos Passos, *1919,* New York, Harcourt, Brace, 1932, pp. 100, 9.

4. André Bazin, *What Is Cinema,* Berkeley and Los Angeles, University of California Press, 1967, p. 64.

5. J. D. Salinger, *Franny and Zooey,* Boston and Toronto, Little, Brown, 1961, pp. 74–75.

6. Vladimir Nabokov, "The Assistant Producer," in *Nabokov's Dozen,* New York, Doubleday, 1958, pp. 75, 76, 77.

7. Heinrich Böll, *Tomorrow and Yesterday,* New York, Criterion, 1957, pp. 24–25.

8. James Agee, *A Death in the Family,* New York, McDowell Obolensky, 1957, pp. 17–19.

9. Malcolm Lowry, *Under the Volcano,* New York, Vintage, 1958, p. 48.

10. Alain Robbe-Grillet, *The Voyeur,* New York, Grove Press, 1958, p. 3.

11. Arnold Hauser, *The Social History of Art,* Vol. 2, New York, Knopf, 1951, p. 939.

12. Norman Mailer, *The Naked and the Dead,* New York, Holt, Rinehart and Winston, 1948, p. 100.

13. Ezra Pound, *The ABC of Reading*, New York, New Directions, 1960, p. 76.

7 / THE QUESTION OF ORDER AND COHERENCE IN POETRY AND FILM

1. Vachel Lindsay, *The Art of the Moving Picture*, New York, Macmillan, 1915, p. 254.
2. Hart Crane, *The Complete Poems of Hart Crane*, New York, Doubleday (Anchor), 1958, pp. 78, 3.
3. E. A. Robinson, *Collected Poems*, New York, Macmillan, 1929, p. 94.
4. Wallace Stevens, *The Collected Poems of Wallace Stevens*, New York, Knopf, 1961, p. 19.
5. St. John Perse, *Anabasis*, trans. T. S. Eliot, New York, Harcourt, Brace, 1949, pp. 10, 11, 25.
6. William Carlos Williams, *The Collected Earlier Poems*, New York, New Directions, 1951, p. 407.
7. Robert Frost, *Complete Poems of Robert Frost*, New York, Henry Holt, 1959, p. 443.
8. Stevens, p. 76.
9. Archibald MacLeish, *Collected Poems, 1917–1952*, Boston, Houghton Mifflin, 1952, p. 41.
10. Richard Wilbur, *Things of This World*, New York, Harcourt, Brace, 1956, p. 8.
11. Frank Kermode, *New York Review of Books*, Vol. 2, No. 1, February 20, 1964, p. 1.
12. Michael Drayton, *The Works of Michael Drayton*, Vol. 2, ed. J. W. Hebel, Oxford, Blackwell, 1961, p. 341.
13. Williams, p. 277.

8 / WASTE LANDS: THE BREAKDOWN OF ORDER

1. W. B. Yeats, *The Collected Poems of W. B. Yeats*, New York, Macmillan, 1955, pp. 184–185.
2. Robert Frost, *Complete Poems of Robert Frost*, New York, Henry Holt, 1959, p. 396.
3. T. S. Eliot, *The Complete Poems and Plays*, New York, Harcourt, Brace, 1952, p. 128.

4. Quoted by Lillian Ross in *The New Yorker*, Oct. 30, 1965, p. 66.
5. Eliot, p. 52.
6. Ibid., p. 44.
7. Ibid., p. 3.
8. Federico Fellini, *La Dolce Vita*, New York, Ballantine Books, 1961, p. 1.
9. Eliot, p. 38.
10. Ibid., pp. 5, 24.
11. Ibid., p. 41.
12. Ibid., p. 39.
13. Ibid., p. 7.
14. Ibid., p. 58.
15. Miguel de Unamuno, *Tragic Sense of Life*, New York, Dover, 1954, p. 268.
16. Alfred North Whitehead, *The Function of Reason*, Boston, Beacon Press, 1958, introductory summary.
17. Nathanael West, *The Complete Works of Nathanael West*, New York, Farrar, Strauss and Cudahy, 1957, p. 104.
18. E. M. Forster, "Art for Art's Sake" in *Modern Culture and the Arts*, ed. Hall and Ulanov, New York, McGraw-Hill, 1967, p. 24.

9 / The Survival of Humanism

1. Béla Balázs, *Theory of the Film*, London, Dennis Dobson, 1953, pp. 39, 41.
2. Ibid., pp. 42–43.
3. George Steiner, *Language and Silence*, New York, Atheneum, 1967, p. 101.
4. Paul Fussell, Jr., *Poetic Meter and Poetic Form*, New York, Random House, 1965, pp. 4–5.
5. W. B. Yeats, *The Collected Poems of W. B. Yeats*, New York, Macmillan, 1955, p. 336.
6. Edwin Muir, *Collected Poems of Edwin Muir*, New York, Grove Press, 1957, p. 143.
7. Ezra Pound, *The Cantos*, New York, New Directions, 1948, Canto LXXXI, pp. 98–99.
8. T. S. Eliot, *The Complete Poems and Plays*, New York, Harcourt, Brace, 1952, p. 125.
9. Wallace Stevens, *The Collected Poems of Wallace Stevens*, New York, Knopf, 1961, pp. 129–130.

10. Eliot, pp. 121, 145.
11. Ibid., p. 121.
12. Ibid., p. 145.
13. Béla Balázs, p. 168.
14. Cesare Zavattini, "Some Ideas on the Cinema," in *Film: A Montage of Theories,* ed. MacCann, New York, Dutton, 1966, p. 218, and Stanley Kauffmann, A *World on Film,* New York, Harper and Row, 1966, p. 420.
15. Parker Tyler, *The Three Faces of the Film,* New York, Thomas Yoseloff, 1960, pp. 143–144.
16. Carl Dreyer, "Thoughts on my Craft," in *Film: A Montage of Theories,* p. 313.
17. V. I. Pudovkin, *Film Technique and Film Acting,* London, Vision: Mayflower, 1958, p. 25.
18. Vachel Lindsay, *The Art of the Moving Picture,* New York, Macmillan, 1915, p. 193.
19. Alexis de Tocqueville, *Democracy in America,* Oxford, London, New York and Toronto, Oxford University Press, 1946, Ch. 23, p. 342.

Index

A NOTE ON THE TYPE

The text of this book was set on the Linotype in ELECTRA, a twentieth-century roman designed by W. A. Dwiggins (1880–1956). Electra is light in color, slightly compressed, and combines the gradual transitions of old-style types with the flat serifs of the so-called "moderns." The design can be traced directly to W.A.D.'s vigorous calligraphy, a feature of many of the finest books and bindings of recent years.

The book was composed by *Service Typographers, Inc.*, Indianapolis Ind.; printed by *The Murray Printing Company*, Forge Village, Mass.; and bound by *Haddon Craftsmen, Inc.*, Scranton, Pa.

Designed by *Guy Fleming*.